It Began in Transylvania

A MEMOIR OF MISTAKES AND SURPRISES

Renee Palmer

© 2015 Renee Palmer
All rights reserved.

ISBN: 1517604613
ISBN 13: 9781517604615

Contents

Introduction ··· xi
Family Background ·· 1
    Mother ··· 2
    Father ·· 10
Life in Romania 1950-1962 ·· 15
    The house ·· 16
    The river Styx under our house ································· 19
    The winter outhouse ·· 20
    Horses ·· 21
    Winter Shoes ·· 22
    How to choose a bride ·· 24
    Drunken crimes ·· 26
    35 Potato Pancakes ·· 27
    Sleeping with pigs ··· 29
    Mice ··· 30
    Entertainment ·· 34
    Stela's cemetery ·· 38
    Arrested at 8 ·· 40
The beginning of the end ··· 42
    My father in the armoire ··· 42
    Winning (and un-winning) the math prize ··················· 45
    The wrath and power of the political party ·················· 47
    Ratzele and the brassieres ·· 48
    Expelled from school ··· 49

Leaving Romania · 53
   First Interpreter Job on Tarom Airline · 54
   Landing in Vienna· ·55
Welcome to New York ·59
   Early Academic Disappointments ·61
   Jamaica High School ·63
   "Prostitutes" in Jamaica High School· ·65
   Other Social Fails · 66
   Adelphi University· ·69
   Queens College ·70
Wacky Trips· ·73
   Israel – week after the 6 Day War 1967 ·73
   France 1968-1969 · 77
   Nancy - France ·78
   Border problems – or The Never-ending Train Rides· · · · · · · · · · · ·81
   Snow wreckage ·85
   The pig in the suitcase ·89
   I was (almost) a spy · 90
   Kent State University crisis· 94
   Plane crash in Newfoundland · 97
   My Wedding in France 1970 ·100
France 1970-1972· ·104
   French Police ·108
   Romania 1972· 114
   Casablanca· ·120
   East Hampton ·121
Marriages· 125
Jobs · 133
   Temp Jobs · 133
   Fashion Industry Jobs · 139
   Christian Dior· 139
   Yves Saint Laurent ·146
   Coach Leatherware · 149

Halston Handbags	159
Mark Cross	165
Hermès	171
The Bedford Impersonation	174
The 1989 San Francisco earthquake	176
Frankly Fake Finishes	183
Technology phase	191
Fashion Group International	194
IBM	199
Haute Cuisine Cockroaches	205
Pink Rat	210
Letters	212
Personality traits	220
Boy, was my father in an armoire!	222
Takeaway	227
Acknowledgements	231
References	233

The most important thing for everyone in Gringolandia is to have ambition and become "somebody", and frankly, I don't have the least ambition to become anybody.

Frida Kahlo

Introduction

I BEGAN THIS MEMOIR IN 1997. I started by writing a rambling series of vignettes about life growing up in Transylvania. The main reason for jotting down these stories was because, though nobody ever said it to my face, I think lots of my friends, or even acquaintances, have viewed me as kind of … how shall I say, odd, bizarre and definitely "different". But then maybe I am …. bizarre.

Here's one example of how I don't conform to typical New York behavior. While most in the city will freak out at the sight of the dreaded cockroach, a skittering mouse, and the rare but scary bat, none of this bothers me in the slightest. As you read my story you'll see why.

But why would it take me 18 years to write this stuff? It didn't take that long – I just kept dropping the project for months, then sometime years as I got involved in other things, like life.

What finally propelled me to finish it is an astounding discovery I just made about my father after a trip back to my home town in Romania in 2013. It was the revelation of a 65-year old family secret that came to light through pure chance when I ran into some childhood friends during my trip.

That bombshell prompted me to finish what I started 18 years ago. My vignettes are comical, preposterous, sad, some really stupid but I hope mostly colorful. For the uninitiated reader, I think it is impossible to appreciate some of the events described here, if one is not familiar with what it's like being Jewish, the first born child of Holocaust survivors who after the war lived under an oppressive totalitarian government, namely post-war communist Romania, in the most backward – almost medieval – conditions.

As in all life there is nature and nurture, the nature part cannot be avoided; the nurture part ultimately defines our personalities. Considering the trifecta of the conditions above, it is a miracle that my generation and I are not more damaged and have even thrived.

But my best early memories are still from my hometown in Romania, because however medieval, it was a pastoral life.

And let's get one thing out of the way lest I disappoint anybody – there is no mention of bats Dracula or other ridiculous Hollywood inventions involving Transylvania. Yes, we had bats, like every other country, and just like the bats on our fire escape in New York City. The only connection with bats that I remember is that if you found a dead bat on the ground, you hung it up on your front door for a while. It was supposed to bring good luck.

Family Background

My family was born in Romania, in the county of Maramureș which is part of Transylvania.

Though my parents did not know each other before the war, they were both deported in 1944 to concentration camps, but from different locations. My mother was 22 and lived in Sighet, where she was born; my father was 30 and lived in Galați, some 300 miles away from where he was born, in Borșa.

Before the war, Sighet was a bustling lively small town with a substantial Jewish population of about 8,000 people living somewhat comfortably among the majority Hungarian population.

Borșa, on the other hand, was a small village at the foot of the Carpathian Mountains and though there was a large number of Jewish families, it was predominantly a rural population consisting of people who subsisted by selling their crops, livestock and various agricultural by-products. For example, once a week, a woman would come down from the mountains with pots filled with water which covered large balls of butter and my mother and other families, would buy a slice of butter. Some men worked in the gold and silver mines outside the village or in the lumber business while others were tradesmen or craftsmen like tailors, shoemakers, etc.

Figure 1- Left: mom's Davidovich family, circa 1927; Right: dad's Schneider family, circa 1928

MOTHER

My mother's family in Sighet was in the textile business. Her father, Jacob Davidovich, had a textile factory and a store selling the fabrics used in traditional Romanian national costumes - a white woolen fabric that was the basis of every Romanian's wardrobe – embroidered peasant blouses and skirts for women, and tunics and pants for men. In retrospect, it's ironic that all the machinery was German, a harbinger of things to come.

We also know that my mother's family was a large clan named Zola originating in Spain and expelled during the Inquisition. In fact, I was told that sometime in the 1930s, my great-grandfather Josef Zola, received a letter from someone (we never found out who) in Cordoba inviting him to bring his family back to Spain. Though the Franco regime was an ally of Germany before and during the war, Spain never gave up its Jews to the Nazis. Rumor has it that Franco was from a "converso" Jewish family. Not quite sure what the purpose of that letter was but in retrospect, maybe it was a warning my family didn't heed. They stayed put!

Speaking of the Zola and Davidovich families, I was told about some amusing relatives. On the Zola side, it's Jean Lafitte, the famous French-American pirate in the 1800s. Lafitte was actually a Zola on his mother's side. They were a Spanish family that escaped to France after being forced to become "conversos".

On the Davidovich side, it's the late Edward G. Robinson who was a second cousin.

My mother's family certainly has some interesting ancestors – a pirate and an actor best known for playing gangsters.

The geography of our part of Romania is confusing even to someone from the region. In the '30s it was Romania but before 1920 it was Hungary. So whereas my mother, born in Sighet in 1922 was born in Romania, her siblings also born in Sighet before 1920, were born in Hungary. This corner of Europe, part of the Austro-Hungarian Empire, was always the prize that went to the winner after each war. The borders kept changing so the nationality of people in any town depended on the year in question and who won the last war - totally confusing to outsiders and even to residents.

We know from my mother about some of the horrors before they were taken away in the cattle cars.

Before the deportation in 1944, the family was thrown out of their house at 80 Bogdan Voda in Sighet and moved into a ghetto for several months. This ghetto comprised a number of streets that the Hungarians who were running the town at the time, under the command of the Germans, designated as the only area where Jews could live. Also, at that time, all Jews were ordered to wear a Yellow Star of David. While in the ghetto, they shared a house with another family, so there were about 11 people in one house. They were also forced to work in various parts of the city, manual labor that was imposed on them by the Hungarians who forced them to do factory work, road work, whatever.

The night before they were carted away to the camps, all the Jewish men were rounded up in the synagogue. Nobody knows exactly what went on there, only horrific screams were heard all over the city. When they were released the next day, my grandfather's face was indescribable, his eyes were red and his black beard had turned completely white overnight.

The following day, they were told they were going to work camps and to pack just necessary things. It was early morning and the city was quiet. The streets were empty and the only sound was the sound of shoes on the asphalt, people walking - hordes of people walking, holding bags and babies and little children. The Hungarian residents watched secretly behind their curtains as these rows of people marched silently by with no sound except the thud of shoes on the ground. What were they thinking?

The Germans made the Jews walk several kilometers to a railroad filled with cattle cars and forced them all in. I can't describe what went on there. My mother documented it in a video made in 1995. Of course, these events and similar horrors have been written about and filmed many times, but this is what happened to MY family.

My mother always remembers that when they arrived in Auschwitz everyone was commanded to leave all their baggage — an immense collection of beautiful and expensive luggage, bags of jewelry and other valuables which made sense since people were told to take only their most precious possessions as they were being moved to another country.

The Nazis sure were smart – they had the Jews bring their valuables themselves, no need to ransack their houses for jewelry, just paintings!

As I mentioned, my mother and part of her family were deported to Auschwitz in May 1944. I say part of the family because one older brother and sister had left before the war and lived in New York. In fact, that brother, Leibi Davidovich, who changed his name to Louis Davis was drafted into the American army and was stationed in England before D-day but was not part of the landing in France.

The horror of the year spent in Auschwitz is indescribable. I leave that to historians. But here are just a few details about my mother's personal experience.

For example, I am named in memory of a 14 year old girl Renike who died at my mother's side in Auschwitz. In Hungarian, Renike is a diminutive for Reni, like Charlie is for Charles. The origin of my name is monstrous and disturbing but I need to tell about it.

Every night, in the freezing winter, the camp guards would call all the women from the barracks and make them stand naked outside from 2AM to 4AM. Some women fainted and were shot. Others just collapsed and died. They would then call out 3 random names. As the women stepped forward, they were shot on the spot. Everything was random, like a lottery game. That's how Renike's mother was killed right in front of her. After that my mother decided to watch over the poor girl and one night as they were running to shelter during a bombing, my mother holding this girl's hand, saw her hit by a bomb, her insides blown out in front of her while my mother was still holding the girl's hand – only with no body attached.

Another type of selection process, this time with a happy ending for my mother's family was Dr. Mengele's regular inspection to decide whether the women prisoners were fit to work or were to be gassed immediately. This also entailed standing naked outside in front of Mengele as he inspected every woman's body for any signs of weakness or frailty. My mother's sister Frida was such a person, shorter than her two other sisters, much skinnier and rather frail. She was therefore pulled away from the line of healthy prisoners and placed in the "death line". Fortunately, at some point during the process, as Mengele turned away for a moment, the two sisters grabbed Frida from the other line and took her back to their group. The whole thing took about 30 seconds, and that saved her life. It is awe-inspiring that in that terrifying atmosphere they risked their lives to save Frida and that the women who saw this rescue kept marching to their deaths without saying a word. There are no words to describe this type of sacrifice.

While we are all too familiar with survivors' horror stories, there is one story of bravery and ingenuity that has never been told: my mother, along with several of her fellow prisoners are among the unsung heroes of the war, the kind of story that gets lost in the din of the unspeakable atrocities.

One of the slave labor camps where my mother and her sisters were forced to work was an ammunitions factory in Somerda that built bombs on an assembly line. My mother and her sister Frida worked on the assembly line, while her other sister Pepci was working in another part of the factory where she was measuring grenades. If the grenades were the correct size (about 12 inches long and 3 inches wide) they were put on the assembly line. If the size was off, they were thrown into a disposal container.

My mother and her sister Frida worked on the assembly line that produced the bombs. There, another woman prisoner who happened to be an engineer discovered that a certain pin they were supposed to fasten into each bomb was the trigger that detonated the bomb. She proceeded to whisper to the woman next to her how to twist the pin so that it would not engage, in essence creating a dud. That woman then whispered it to the next woman and so on until all the women on the assembly line were in on the scam.

So, for 2 months, these women, risking their lives, sabotaged an entire production run of bombs that were destined for the allied forces as they were closing in at the end of the war. Had they been discovered, they would have been shot on the spot.

My mother's parents were murdered in Auschwitz. Also killed was my mother's sister Sari (pronounced Shaari) who was the only one married at the time, with 2 children. She was killed because she did not want to be separated from her children. Her husband, Shlomo Fruchter survived and since his family was originally from Borşa, he returned there after being liberated.

My mother and her sisters were liberated in May 1945 by the Soviet Army during the death marches away from the camps. They were finally liberated in Brno, Czechoslovakia, today the Czech Republic. I was told that the Czechs were incredibly kind and welcoming, opening their houses and businesses to these liberated prisoners and showering them with food, clothing and other sustenance. Maybe it's because the Czechs were the first victims of Nazi aggression – who knows? All we know is that they were wonderful people. The Russians then returned them to Sighet, their home town.

Since one of the sisters, Frida, was married before she was deported, she was re-united with her husband in Czechoslovakia after the liberation and remained there, in Usti Nad Labem where their son, Robert, was born in October 1946.

My mother, upon her return to Sighet with her sister Pepci was asked to go to Borşa where her surviving brother-in-law, Shlomo Fruchter introduced her to my father and they soon were engaged and then married on November 20, 1945.

Figure 2- My parents wedding, November 20, 1945.

Pepci attended my mother's wedding and then tried to figure out how to get out of the country. There was no real rush but what contributed to her desire to get away was the fact that she got sort of creeped out when she learned that her surviving brother-in-law, the same Shlomo Fruchter who introduced my mother to my father, wanted to marry her. It is a common old Jewish custom for men to marry their brothers' widows but my aunt was just not into that. Which was a good decision since Shlomo ended up marrying another woman but eventually went insane after a couple of years and passed away. The insanity of course, came from the camp experience. We knew of several people, mostly men, who went insane a few years after liberation.

Enter my uncle Leibi (renamed Louis), the one who was in the American army stationed in England and who was shipped back to the US after D-Day. He asked to be allowed to return to Europe to look for his sisters since they were liberated by the Russians and not the Americans. Prisoners who were liberated by the Americans were allowed to emigrate immediately to the US, while the Russians sent everyone back to their original hometowns.

Since Pepci was the only one who wasn't married by then, Louis brought her back to the US as his war bride on the U.S.S Gripsholm, a military ship. She changed her name to Joan. They got divorced quite quickly and she married my uncle Micki, also from Sighet, whom she met in Paris while waiting with her brother to board the ship in Calais for the voyage to New York. Micki was also waiting for a visa to the US but the only visa he got was to Nicaragua. Go figure. He nevertheless ended up in the US where he looked up my aunt and they got married.

One other sibling, my mother's older brother Eugene, was first in a Hungarian army work camp. When the Germans took over the area, he was transferred to the German army, not the SS, just the army. This was in the region called Trei Scaune (Three Seats) and specifically Scaunul Ciuc (The Ciuc Seat) which was a medieval Romanian/Hungarian administrative area much like counties in the U.S. These regional seats were established in 1324, and the origin of the names is still unknown, though it is believed that they come from Turkish, where *Ciuc* means "border" or "border mountain".

Some of the tasks my uncle and the others in the work camp were forced to perform were such incredibly crippling labor that they just couldn't take it and many of them simply deserted and ran across several cities such as Dej and Beclean to end up in Oradea, in 1944.

Since the Russians had already taken over that area, they were told by a Russian officer to simply return to their home town of Sighet.

That they did and then another bizarre event took place.

At that time there were barely 60 surviving Jews in Sighet, from the original 8,000 before the war. The Russian general who ran the city had a Hungarian girlfriend. She told him that the Jews came back from the camps to rob everybody in the city. The reality was that they only tried to go back to their old homes from which they were first evicted into the ghetto area before being deported to the camps.

Their homes were of course taken over by local Hungarians when all the Jews were carted away. Needless to say, the new occupants of all these ill-gotten houses were not in the mood to give up their new abodes so the Russian general, on advice of his Hungarian girlfriend, rounded up all these surviving Jews who returned home and declared them prisoners of war. They were shipped off to the Ukraine where they were held until 1947. For the following 2 years they wandered from the Ukraine to Romania and my uncle eventually reached Borșa and met my mother, my father and me — I was 2 years old.

He then decided to try to go to the U.S. where his older brother, Louis and older sister Regina lived. He crossed Romania to Hungary and Czechoslovakia where he reunited with his sister Frida and her husband Ari and continued to Germany. At the German border he was met by a

Jewish group from the newly established state of Israel who helped surviving European Jews go to what was then called Palestine. But my uncle wanted to go to the U.S. where the rest of his family was so the Israelis helped him get to Munich and after a year and half wait with his younger brother Eddie, in January 1949 they emigrated to the U.S. under the Truman Statement and Directive on Displaced Persons. The odd thing which I kept asking about was why Eddie's surname in the US was Zola, instead of Davidovich, or the Americanized version, Davis. Turns out that Eddie had lost all his papers and had no documentation about his identity. So his uncle Morris Zola in the US, told him to say that he was Morris's brother and that's how Eddie got into the US.

Small digression: when I was 10 I lived in Sighet for a while with my mother, who gave birth to my sister, while my father was in prison in Sighet. During this time, an aunt, Molvi néni, (the Hungarian version of Aunt Molvi) took me to the family house at 80 Bogdan Voda Street. The Hungarian family who lived there at the time allowed us in when my aunt explained that she just wanted to show me what my mother's family house looked like. The current owners were amiable and let us in. I was too young to appreciate what I saw other than the ceiling which left an impression on me even at that young age. It was beautifully painted, like synagogue or church ceilings. That ceiling is about all I remember of my mother's family's house.

FATHER

We don't know much about my father's family other than the fact that his father died when my father and his twin brother were about 4 years old. We also know that my grandmother didn't like my grandfather much because he used to hide in the attic and write poetry. He was an artist, a dreamer, which was not very useful when you had to manage your property, livestock and other household duties. My father also had 2 older sisters, Mantzi and Pepi and an older brother Manya, who died in the camps.

I also know that their father changed the family name from Schorr to Schneider because he wanted to avoid sounding Jewish. Needless to say, when I was told about this, I couldn't stop laughing. That's like changing your name from dick to prick. But I guess at that time, Schneider sounded more German than Jewish.

I don't know if there was any relation here, but it is known that Friedrich Schorr, who was Jewish, was a renowned baritone of Wagnerian opera in Germany and his father was a cantor at a synagogue. It is therefore possible that my grandfather simply wanted to atone for the artistic blunder of this Schorr person for singing Wagner operas since Wagner was Hitler's favorite composer. Ok, I doubt that but it sounds interesting.

Personally, not only is Wagner tainted for me for being liked by Hitler, which obviously is not his fault, but most Wagner operas are so depressing, and the music so ominous, I could never sit through any of them. Ok, I do like Tristan und Isolde but that's it. I'm glad Hitler wasn't an avid lover of Beethoven, Mozart, Bach or any other of my favorite German composers which would really ruin my obsession with Baroque and classical music.

My father was a Talmudic scholar. He was apparently so smart when he was a little boy, that the Jewish community in Borşa decided that he must be helped to continue his studies in a yeshiva in Galaţi. Since his mother did not have the money to send him away, the community got together and raised the money to send him to a yeshiva in Galaţi.

While at the yeshiva, like all the other students, or as they called them, *yeshiva bocheren,* he had room and board at the school during the week but had to find ways to eat on Friday night and Saturday.

The practice was called "eating days" and it consisted of finding Jewish families that would feed him on Friday night and Saturday. In exchange, he had to sing and conduct the Shabbat ceremonies at that family's house. He hated every minute of it, never grew a beard, mustache or sideburns (*peyes*.) He just rejected the whole concept, but was fascinated with learning Jewish law. This had nothing to do with religion; it was all about the rules of humanity.

Figure 3- In the army: dad and twin brother Moisi with friend, dad relaxing with book, circa 1935

After he returned from the yeshiva in the early 1930s he was drafted into what I believe was the Hungarian army. Apparently, while in the army, he spent his free time reading. In 1944, he was deported to a labor camp in Poland where he cleaned latrines and polished the boots of German officers. After he finished, the officers would kick him in the head with their freshly polished boots, in lieu of thanks, I guess.

My father and his brother came back to Borşa and so did his sisters, Mantzi and Pepi. Mantzi and her husband who also survived, left immediately for Israel via Malta. My father, his brother Moishi and sister Pepi remained in Borşa.

Unlike the Hungarians from Sighet who occupied all the Jews's houses when they were deported, the people in Borşa did no such thing. All Jewish homes were left intact so those who returned from the camps found everything the way it was left. The Christians of Borşa were angels.

Regarding my father's Talmudic training, though he outwardly didn't look like or follow the practices of religious Jews, he still believed deeply in the laws, ideology and doctrines which are the basis of modern Western society. But the issue of God was not in the equation. He was in fact a confirmed atheist. So you could say he was an atheistic Talmudic scholar – an interesting oxymoron. Maybe his beliefs in a supreme being were changed after the Holocaust. I remember once asking him something about God, and his answer was, "There is no God. No God would allow what happened". What he was instead was an ardent Zionist, and had he been able to leave Romania after I was born, we would have been in Israel where he had a job waiting for him in the government under formation in 1948. But my mother didn't want to travel with a small baby, so they stayed in Borşa where they got trapped for 15 years.

My parents were the first of his family to get married. I was born in February 1947 in Sighet because the doctor who delivered me, a family relative, lived in Sighet. After a few weeks, they came back to Borşa and I believe I was among the first post-war babies born in our village as shown in the photo below. I am the second from the right, with the bow on my head. It was a show of triumph for these women who survived the Holocaust – the re-generation.

*Figure 4 – Left: Baby boomers, baby Renee with bow;
Right: Mom, dad and baby Renee, 1947*

Life in Romania 1950-1962

THOUGH THE COMMUNIST REGIME TOOK over about a year after I was born, the first few years, before I started school, were some of the happiest times of my life. Living in the country and being allowed to run around like a wild animal was simply paradise, and in retrospect it is the reason why I'm obviously so attached to Romania. The local people in Borşa were simple but extraordinarily kind and hospitable.

It was a really primitive region. We traveled by horse and buggy or cow drawn carts full of hay. There were chickens, geese, goats, sheep and other animals everywhere, on the roads and on private properties. Fortunately, to my delight, these animals are still there today in between the Mercedes, Audis, Fiats and Dacias (a Romanian version of the Renault).

Though most of this happened in the 1950s, in retrospect life there was in so many ways closer to the Middle Ages than the 20th century. There were a few odd habits which I think are really peculiar to this region as it was rather backward and quite isolated from the rest of the country by treacherous mountain roads and frigid weather, especially in the winter.

I spent the first 15 years of my life under the evolving Communist regime until we left in 1962. I say "evolving" because when I was a child in school, the head of the country was Georghe Georghiu-Dej. Several years before we left the country, Nicolae Ceausescu became more visible and important. I don't know exactly when the transition took place, I'm sure it is well documented but to me it was part of an evolving persecution, as Ceausescu started implementing the most oppressive and corrupt government and my family was one of the key targets.

For example, the systematic disappearance of people because someone overheard someone else say something anti-government and ratted them out to the police was always a cloud hanging over people's heads. I remember one such incident from around 1960, when Ceausescu announced an amnesty for all political prisoners, probably because there wasn't enough room in the prisons anymore what with judges who gave out 100 year sentences for ridiculous infractions. There was much happiness as people started to come home. Then one day, a friend of my father's, while having a drink in a bar, said something to the effect that, "yeah, they let them out now, and then they'll arrest them again tomorrow." The man disappeared the next day and was never heard from again. We left the country a few years later.

So the only element of my upbringing that had a lasting negative impact on me was that children could not ask their parents questions. Typical questions that had to do with our way of life were always answered with "don't ask questions like this." Why? "Because." It all had to do with fear of government retribution but of course that was never explained. Obviously this had to do with the fact that kids talk, and when kids talked, their parents tended to disappear, usually in the middle of the night.

But it was still the best part of my life. Here are just a few adventures from my childhood as a country bumpkin.

THE HOUSE
Our house, as most of the houses in the village, was on the main street which at that time was named Strada Principala (Main Street). It was across the street from a "grocery" store named *Alimentara* whose shelves were always empty, but more about that later.

The house was a rather large L-shaped structure but primitive as all houses were in rural areas at the time. There were five rooms and a larder in the middle, at the right angle point. After my aunt Pepi and her husband moved into our house, the larder, about the size of a modern walk-in closet with a stair case to the attic separated our "apartment" from that of my aunt. She must have gotten married about three years after my father because I remember being in the room she later occupied as my bed was next to the wall that separated the room from the larder.

Children remember the oddest things even at a very young age. I remember eating the white paint off the walls from my crib; it was some kind of whitewash. I think I was calcium deficient.

After Pepi got remarried, having lost her first husband in the camps, she and her new husband had no place to live, so my father gave her half the house. One funny thing was her husband's name – Max Brettschneider. Our name was Schneider. It must have been funny for her to go from Schneider to Brettschneider. Schneider means tailor (fabric cutter), while Brettschneider means woodcutter. Still a "cutter", but what kind? I assume it had something to do with the lumber business which was and still is the main industry in that area.

We had electricity, intermittent - sometimes on, sometimes off; a yellow glazed terracotta stove like a column that rose up almost to the ceiling for heating the room and a low black iron stove for cooking. There was no bathroom or toilet, or running water – we got water from a fountain on the street and carried it home in buckets.

To take a bath or wash dishes, there were portable metal sinks and metal bathtubs. You heated the water in a pot on the stove and then poured it into the sink or bathtub. Taking a bath was a two-person affair – someone had to pour water over you to rinse out the soap. We also collected rain water which was great for washing hair. At some point, around 1955, my parents installed a water pump in the living room so we could pump water and did not have to go to the well anymore. Cold water, of course.

We had a back yard with an outhouse, a chicken coop/stable for various livestock and a vegetable garden that extended up to the bank of the Vişeu River. That was the end of the property.

The house, though quite well built and certainly more elaborate than a hut, unfortunately had the same amenities as a hut – none. Sort of like the 17th century "chateau" I lived in years later in France when I had to go to a friend's house to take a shower.

We all survived on vegetables from the garden and meat from livestock that everybody had. Of course, I didn't know about the meat until the unfortunate episode with the pig – more about this later—hope you're keeping notes -- after which my parents had to buy meat from various people who came down from the mountains peddling meat and butter. We no longer could have livestock because of me.

Clothing was made from sheared sheep wool and shoes were rectangular shaped pieces of leather folded over the foot, and held in place with strips of leather. These were called "opinci" and were worn mostly in the summer. In the winter, we wore boots, also hand made, but only used by the locals. We each had one pair of shoes made by a shoemaker. There were only two stores for clothes which, as I remember, were mostly always empty, a pharmacy and a pastry shop that had nice cakes, and an Alimentara, which was the grocery store – all the shelves always empty except for sacks of flour and rice.

In truth, money couldn't buy anything; there was nothing to buy unless one traveled out of the area to a larger city whose stores were a little more stocked with merchandise.

But I remember that even in Bucharest, when there was meat at the butcher shops, you had to stand on line from early morning and by the time it was your turn, they had run out of meat and all they had were bones. So you bought the bones and made soup.

In terms of food, we fared much better in the countryside since we all had gardens and livestock. Though I wish I didn't know about livestock. To me they were pets.

THE RIVER STYX UNDER OUR HOUSE

One of the oddest things about our house was how it was built. I never asked my parents why the house was built like this because, as I mentioned before, questions were taboo.

All I knew was that the house belonged to my father's uncle who did not return from the concentration camp and it had still been under construction at the time he was deported because there were some obvious elements of a typical house that had not yet been put into place, like steps to the front door. We had to climb on rocks to reach the front door until my parents built a veranda for access and hanging out.

At the back of the L-shaped house was a strange, perfectly arched opening just like a tunnel. It looked as though it was built so you could walk under the house all the way to the front, though there was no exit onto the street so there was no light at the end of the tunnel. Pardon the pun. Also, you really couldn't walk in this tunnel because it was filled with a very dark and mysterious looking greasy liquid. We had something like a mysterious lake under the house.

Maybe there was something left to be built, like a foundation. I don't know. But since the floorboards in the house were not well laid, with no foundation, the water kept eating away at the floorboards and there were gaping holes between them through which you could see the below. I used to look through those gaps and every time I did, I saw eyes staring back at me. I had no idea what they were – fish, frogs, snakes – who knows. But there were definitely some creatures under the house.

Then, a few years later, some weeds came through the wood planks and within a year we had a bush growing in the middle of the living room, from under the wood planks. The bush ultimately grew into a real tree and nobody paid any attention to it – go figure. I guess under the circumstances, the hardships and persecution, who cared about a tree of indeterminate origin growing in the living room. Over the years I've seen such built-in trees in mega-mansions in The Hamptons so I'm proud to say that we had such a tree in 1957 in our pathetic house in the Carpathian Mountains! So there!

THE WINTER OUTHOUSE

Another feature that no Hamptons mansion can possibly claim to have is an outhouse with resident wolves in the backyard.

The problem with the outhouse was that if you had "to go" on a cold winter night, you ended up having to hold it in because the wolves were howling right next to the outhouse. They were very brazen as they came as close as 100 feet from the house. You could see their eyes shine in the moonlight, eager for a snack. So you waited until the morning. Our house was separated from the mountains of the village by a river so I assume they swam across the river in order to end up in our backyard. Oh, I also love wolves, they are beautiful. But I wasn't ready to be their dinner.

Speaking of wolves, there was another issue with the outhouse in the winter. This may be a bit crass but there was something amusing about it, well, at least it was amusing to me. In the summer there was no problem except for the dozens of daddy-long-leg spiders which were all over the inside walls. I have always been afraid of spiders but these guys didn't bother me that much because they didn't move. It's just that it was a bit freaky, because they looked like three-dimensional wallpaper.

On the other hand, in the winter, while there were no spiders, there was an issue involving the laws of physics and chemistry. The issue was that this was not an outhouse that you might find even today in various remote country areas, or perhaps camping grounds, where chemistry comes into play as in using chemicals such as lime, to dissolve the mass of human ....hmmmm, "by product".

We didn't have such advanced technology at the time. So there was no maintenance. Therefore in the winter, when the output of the six people using this outhouse froze, it became a three dimensional tower ending in a needle point that often rose out of the hole, above the seat. That means that unless you wanted to risk having your derriere punctured by a peak of frozen caca, you had to come armed with a hammer or an axe to knock down the peak before you could sit down and do your business. Charming, no? I think we all suffered from some form of constipation in the winter, from a combination of howling wolves and the labor involved in the destruction of mountainous dreck.

Horses

The way people were able to get around if they had to go anywhere further than the limits of the village which was about two miles long, was by horse and buggy. Otherwise you went on foot.

One day, in the middle of winter, while we were planning to go somewhere, my parents put me in the horse carriage in the street in front of our house while they went back inside to get something. I was about six or seven years old. It was freezing cold and I was wrapped in blankets and sitting on the back bench.

I don't really remember specifically what caused the accident, but while I was waiting for my parents, the carriage skidded on the ice, probably as the horse was making some movements, and turned over sideways spilling me out into the gutter. When the carriage flipped over, it also dragged the horse, who tripped and fell on top of me.

Fortunately, the horse fell across the gutter with his head and front legs on the sidewalk and his hind legs on the street, with his body covering me like a roof. I think it saved my life!

There was a lot of screaming in the street and people came to help raise the horse, and flip back the cart and get me out of the ravine. Nobody was hurt but I grew a bit terrified of horses since he was thrashing his legs while he was down and it was kind of scary. I did get over it a few years later when I learned to ride horses. But never in the winter!

Winter Shoes

As I said, even if you had money, there was nothing to buy. Clothes had to be made from fabric you bought in any city out of town and the local tailor would then make a dress, or pants, or a coat.

The only benefit from that time in school is that we had to wear a uniform provided by the school, so there wasn't much need for clothes outside of class. The uniform was a navy blue slightly pleated dress with long sleeves and a white collar.

Figure 5- My school uniform, with Shari, 1959

We were also very lucky that during certain times, we were allowed to receive packages from the U.S My mother's family always sent clothes for me when I was a kid. Once they sent me a winter coat that was made of brown fake fur with red woolen trim. It really helped, it was very warm.

The real problem was winter shoes, they were very hard to make so we depended on the shoe store. As for its inventory, it was empty 90% of the time. The other 10% was made up of shoes fit for Big Foot, if such a creature existed.

One winter a large shipment of shoes arrived at the shoe store. How did we know? From the town crier, who walked around the street with a drum announcing such events. So of course, everybody ran to the store, which created endless lines of people waiting. By the time my mother got in, they only had the fake fur lined ankle shoes with a zipper in the front. This would have been OK if they were my size, but the only sizes left were like 10,12, 14 and Big Foot. I cannot imagine who could wear shoes that size, Romanians are not Vikings or Texans, they are average height people.

I ended up with a pair of winter shoes about size 9 which my mother stuffed with cotton at the tip so I could walk without tripping. At that time I was a U.S. size 6. Needless to say, I walked like a duck, but at least my toes weren't freezing. And I was not the only one looking like a clown since all of us had the same shoes.

HOW TO CHOOSE A BRIDE

There was an interesting custom I was told about by many people, but which I have not witnessed myself, and which would have happened only if I were a fly on the wall.

We saw many weddings because they paraded in the street after the church ceremony. This parade was a priest walking in front, the newlyweds and their attendants behind the priest and a horde of people behind them. One of the groomsmen carried a long stick, like a flag, that was decorated with ribbons and bells and kept raising it up and down as they were walking down the street so there was no way to miss this parade. It was really a beautiful custom.

But until you got to an actual wedding, there were a few other steps to consider such as how did the newlyweds get together. Now, it is important to understand that none of us kids had any clue at all about relationships between men and women.

In overhearing adults talking, we kind of figured out what was going on though we had no clue about the role of sex since we had no clue what sex was, as much of the information was clouded in mystery. The custom among the locals was as follows: sometimes, if two families had some money or property, a wedding would be arranged by the parents, just like in other societies around the world.

But people who did not have those kinds of resources were forced into a different path. There was a puritanical custom whereby if an unmarried man was caught having sex with a woman, he had to marry her so most young people, as far as I know, stayed away from such indulgences. Though I really don't know since all those hay carts, barns and other structures away from the main house provided quite a lot of opportunities, if you didn't make too much noise.

If a single guy wanted to get married, he had the option of going to a family that had daughters and a certain ceremony would ensue. Did I mention that Romanians are incredibly hospitable people? This means you didn't have to announce your arrival or ask permission and there was no concept of trespassing. Anybody who came to the door was asked to come in and offered a drink.

The "bachelor" would sit down at the table with the parents and the daughters and any other family members, a bottle of țuica that he brought would be passed around for everybody to take a shot. Sometimes they even poured it into a glass, if they had glasses. The young man would explain in a few words why he was there and then he had the option to "try out" one of the girls. The rest of the family went outside and waited until the couple came out. Then he had the option of trying out another daughter, if he wanted. Let me first emphasize that I had no idea what the "try out" process referred to until years later; I thought it was talking. Duh!

In the end, he picked one, and then came the discussion about a dowry which usually involved an animal or two, wood for the stoves, and sometimes land. Part of the dowry was also pieces of clothing which as I mentioned were all handmade and some, like the *cojoc,* was a beautifully embroidered vest made out of sheepskin.

The embroidery was a very time consuming process as it was very elaborate and intricate, so as soon as a married couple had children, the mom and grandparents started making these vests when the children were born so they would have them ready when the kids were adults. This vest was an indispensable part of the regional costume and so well made that it lasted for years and years. Following the wedding, the couple would go on to have children and they stayed together till death parted them. I never heard of a divorce.

In fact, I never heard of a divorce as long as I lived in Romania. It had nothing to do with the Orthodox religion, It had to do with the concept of accommodation or maybe it was like this in remote rural areas, I don't know. All I know, is people just accommodated each other's idiosyncrasies, whatever they were.

Drunken crimes

Something that I experienced several times between 7-10 years old, and probably several times before but just don't remember, was something that I never told my parents because I knew it wasn't a big deal. This was usually during those times when nobody was home except the maid and I was playing alone in the yard.

It was always a Sunday. On Sundays, many of the locals went to a bar for a drink after church services. It was usually only men and just passing in front of the bar, you could smell alcohol and urine. As it happens, when all you do is drink, eventually fights erupt and all you have to do is utter some insult about "your mother's" something or other, and wham – the fists come out and it's mayhem. Several such fights end up spilling out into the street, and then behind someone's gate into a courtyard.

Since our house was only 2 houses away from such a bar, or *cărciumă*, I witnessed several instances of such drunks coming into our courtyard and finishing each other off, usually by strangling. Even though they saw me staring at them, it didn't matter, as the fights continued. Eventually one man ended up on the ground and I really couldn't tell if he was dead or just badly injured. A few minutes later, several other men would come to get the body out and I never heard about it again.

The first time I told the maid about this, she came out to look but by that time there was no one there. She told me to say nothing, this happens all the time. A few years later, when I was about 10-11, I did ask my father about it and he said basically the same thing. When I asked if this was legal, he said that it shouldn't be but the government didn't care if "these people" killed each other, and the only time you ever got arrested is when you said something against the government. Well, that certainly made sense.

In fact, this wasn't at all unusual because in Țara Oașului, a region not far from our village, it was a weekly occurrence that every Sunday someone got killed during a drunken riot. It was so well known, that if two kids got into a fight in my school, the teachers used to break it up by asking, "Where do you think you are? In Țara Oașului?"

35 POTATO PANCAKES

As I said, my childhood was very happy. Most of it was due to my mother who had no idea how to educate a child, which I assume was the case of all the Jews that returned from the camps. They had no parents or friends with children to guide them.

In fact, until I came to the U.S., I never saw an old Jew. When I was a kid, I thought all Jews were around 30-35 years old, I never saw anybody older than that since obviously they were all killed in the camps and the only ones to survive, like my mother, were those who were able to work.

Be that as it may, the point is that my mother had no clue about raising children. I think the maid showed her how to toilet train me. She then showed my father but since my father was often absent minded, he would put me on the potty while forgetting to take off my pants, which ended in the hysteria from my mother and the maid as I trailed the poop around the house.

But my mother could not be more accommodating to anything I wanted, even at the risk of making me sick. So one day, I think I was around 8-9 years old, she was making potato pancakes (latkes) for dinner. I LOVED potato pancakes, and still do. So as she was frying them, I kept eating them and kept asking for more and more and more, until I ate 35, after which I got really sick, and they had to call the doctor who made me vomit and gave me something to drink which I think was a precursor to Alka-Seltzer. He also told her not to give in to all my food demands in terms of quantity. But I know why she did it: she was happy to see me eat because I was apparently difficult when it came to food, I rejected everything and I remember her friends had to come over to the our house and play games with me to distract me while my mother shoved food in my mouth.

My favorite breakfast was bread and butter with raw onions and chocolate milk. She made it for me every morning. Maybe that's how I developed a cast iron stomach because a few years later when I was taking chemistry in school, I tasted arsenic, belladonna and mercury and all I got was a bit of an upset stomach.

But the best chemistry experiment was in the barn since my mother didn't care what I did as long as I didn't make a mess in the house. This time she was really right.

I don't remember exactly the experiment was but it included sulfuric acid because I remember the stink but there must have been some other chemicals because sulfuric acid does not explode. All I know is that there was a big explosion and flames that sent the chickens flying and I was lucky it didn't spark any flames near the hay loft, or the whole barn would have burned down. I had a burn on my face and fingers that eventually cleared up. My father later suggested that I keep my chemical experiments in school under the supervision of a teacher. But he's the one that bought me the chemistry set so I explained that I was just doing homework. I'm sure they just laughed behind my back, like they always did when I did something stupid – I was never punished for anything, never!

Sleeping with Pigs

No snickering please - this is not one of those singles jokes, though I was single at that time, about 3 years old.

The pig in question was part of our collection of domestic animals and livestock. Except for the pig, all our animals lived on our property. However, because we were Jewish, it was not very cool for us to have a pig so we kept the pig in the neighbor's yard. Their daughter, Emuş (Emilia), though younger than I, was my friend and comrade in arms when we went exploring the property, like sitting on the river bank behind our houses with our feet dangling in the water as the fish nibbled on our skin. It was divine.

I certainly don't remember the details, but apparently I was very attached to this pig and would sneak under the fence to the neighbor's yard looking for him.

Since he would wander around the property, which was quite large extending to the river, I used to wait for him patiently in his trough where I would promptly fall asleep. My parents would of course get hysterical because I had disappeared, though except for being kidnapped by Gypsies, there was no danger to kids wandering around. Of course after much screaming and yelling and an assortment of "oy gevalts" and other "geshries," somebody ended up finding me sleeping with the pig in the trough.

After that first time I understand it became routine – whenever I was missing, they knew where to find me – in the pig's trough.

Then one day, the pig disappeared and I was very upset because nobody would tell me where he was. The other pigs were there, only mine was gone. Eventually I found out and since then I have not eaten pork. It is obvious that I didn't know that livestock was "food" – I thought they were pets since I lived with them in the barn, under the hay stacks and everywhere they were, I was around them.

It was a horrible revelation and I have been in love with pigs ever since.

MICE

"MICE" was the title of this journal when I first started it in 1997, spurred on by the repeated exclamations of disgust whenever the topic was mentioned.

I happen to like mice – actually, no, I love mice. I also love cats which makes for a bit of a problem.

My earliest encounter with these clever little rodents was when I was about 6 or 7 and the local government decided that one room in our house, with its own entrance on the street, would make an excellent granary for the ALIMENTARA, the in-convenience store across the street, in which to warehouse their sacks of flour. As I mentioned, the store had no inventory other than flour, rice and some cans of indeterminate content. But the flour was the most heavily stocked item because it is indispensable for making bread. So without any preamble, the local big cheese bureaucrat came in one day to tell my father that he had to clear away all the furniture from that room so they could use it as storage space for flour.

My father obliged gracefully, in a "take my bedroom, please!" manner. This meant my parents were displaced and so was I, making my sleeping quarters the living room, adjacent the newly designated granary. At the same time, they broke the street wall and built an industrial type door with a vertical **slider**. Now, for those whose only knowledge of a farm is what you saw on Little House on the Prairie, here is a fact of life: flour begets mice.

The festival began one night, about 3 weeks after my parents' former bedroom was turned into a granary.

Figure 6 - Our house with the industrial door

Since my new sleeping quarters in the living room, next to the granary, were separated only by a flimsy door, about 2 inches above the floor, what follows should not be a surprise.

I was sleeping on something like a daybed, with a storage cabinet as the headboard. Therefore, the bed's headboard was a piece of furniture used to display various tchotchkes and the famous telephone. I say famous because, our telephone number was 4 --- yes, just 4.

The reason we even had a telephone is because at that time, my father was a rather prominent figure in our village. He was a member of the Communist party and the director of a lumber business - the Poposală.

The business belonged originally to the Fruchter family, my mother's brother-in-law, who gave it to my father as a wedding present, since he was the matchmaker. My father split it with his brother and the rest of his family. But of course, after the Communists seized it, they gave my father and his brother jobs as directors of the firm. And by the way, if you were invited to join the Communist Party, you accepted with gratitude, or else.

To provide some perspective on my father's standing in the community at that time, I must note that the only other entities possessing a telephone were not mere mortals like my father, but the crème de la crème of local government such as:

The Post Office - Tel #: 1
The Police/Mayor - Tel # : 2
The Electrical Company, Tel #: 3
The Schneider family, Tel #: 4

I don't know if there was a Tel #5. Anyway, this telephone was of the crank type. The phone had this little lever that one turns a few times to elicit a dial tone, which then connected you to the post office operator to whom you would say: "Maria, please give me Comrade Popescu in Bucharest." And she would do it, sometimes.

Figure 7- My father, on the Left with portraits of Marx, Engels, Lenin & Stalin.

Well, the crank lever was a noisy little piece of technology, it rang as you cranked it so if you weren't looking you never knew if the phone was ringing because someone was calling you or ringing because someone was trying to make a call. This marvel rang all the time.

I apologize for this digression, but it is necessary to set stage for the piece de resistance – the nightly concert performed by the ensemble of rodents as they took turns in exercising their little feet on the telephone crank. In retrospect, I believe that they were merely early adopters of the concept of keeping healthy and fit through the use of a treadmill, albeit a musical one, but perhaps this is what inspired them to continue the activity night after night. And yes, they were fit and agile little critters.

The first concert of course woke my parents in a panic. Having the telephone ring at 3 AM is not something they were accustomed to --- after all, who on earth would call in the first place since nobody else in town had a phone except the 3 institutions mentioned above. And why would they call, it was easier to walk over than to wake up the operator: Oh, I forgot to mention that the phone only worked during the day, when Maria the operator was in residence.

So, at the sight of about half a dozen mice prancing around several inches away from my head, my father grinned like a Cheshire cat and my mother started screaming hysterically which frightened the rodents into a hasty retreat to their granary, my parents' former bedroom.

At this point, as horrifying discussions about cheese, traps and poisons ensued, I had to intervene on behalf of the furry ones and beg my parents to leave them alone. I explained in tears that I could not stand for any rodenticide or mistreatment of my friends, my only friends other than Foxy, my dog and my nanny.

I knew what I was doing. Since I was an only child, I used a time tested guilt inducer known as "how come I don't have a brother or sister like my cousin Sofia, and my neighbor Emilia, and Leibi, and Motel and Stela, so I have someone to play with?"

The tactic worked – my parents promised to leave the mice alone to frolic to their hearts' content, and mine. Thereafter, I trained them to come down from the phone shelf over my head, and walk down my body to my feet, where at the edge of the bed, they would jump off and scurry back to their lair, the ultimate restaurant --- an endless supply of food in a variety of grains, and no waiters with attitude. And best of all, it was FREE.

After the nightly training sessions and the benevolence of the 2 legged giants in the house, the creatures became more and more brazen and began to step up the schedule of their appearances. Besides the 3AM gym sessions, they now held scheduled conferences in the middle of the room in the afternoon and early evenings. I don't know what they did in the morning, probably sleeping off their nocturnal exercises, or having long leisurely breakfasts. Suffice it to say, they became a permanent fixture in the household so that when my father's poker buddies would show up for their weekly routine, the mice were part of the setting, just like the refreshments my mother would serve.

I have loved mice ever since and years later, when my cats used to catch them at the country house, I did the unspeakable, unnatural deed of snatching them out of their mouths and putting them out on the deck with the advice to not come back unless they wanted to be lunch for the cats. The lecture was delivered after I kissed them and petted them on the head – with the cat howling in extreme indignation. So I had to appease him with some treats because one cannot disrupt the prey sequence of a cat – it's extremely traumatic and leaves emotional scars causing them to pee on your pillow. After recounting these childhood experiences to my New York friends, is it any wonder that they looked at me in total disgust? I guess not.

ENTERTAINMENT

But, hey, there was a cinema in town which was also the only entertainment. Now, the movies that played here were very interesting. For example, for several years during the early 1950s there was just one movie we saw - *Stalingrad Partea Doua* (Stalingrad Part Two). Don't know what happened to Part One. I guess the Russians were losing. Now this could also have been simply due to living in such a remote area that the last thing the communist regime was worried about was the distribution of movies. I must assume that in Bucharest they saw other movies, I don't know.

By the late 1950's, several years after Stalin died, they started showing new movies which were either Russian or Romanian where the subject was always extolling the virtues of the labor force – so most of them were about happy factory workers singing while they lifted heavy machinery. There were also a number of Indian movies and I'll never forget that the heartthrob of the day was an actor named Raj Kapoor.

The only two American movies I saw were *Spartacus* and *Marty*, probably because both had a political message – the exploitation of the slaves by the imperialist Romans and the exploitation of the working class in the U.S. by the mean capitalists.

One thing that made going to the movies fun is that we would bring our dog Foxy who sat silently at our feet until the audience started laughing at some comedy routine, in which case he would stand up and bark in unison with the audience. If people were crying at some sad scene, Foxy would whimper. My friends were more interested in the dog's reactions than the boring movies, at least they always had something to laugh at. I mean how excited can you get viewing some Romanian movie about cute girls working in a factory on an assembly line? This was not Lucy & Ethel making chocolates, they were making parts for some kind of machinery, like tractors. When they got off from work they went home to celebrate a productive day in the people's factory that produced excellent products for the great Romanian Popular Republic. Yes sir.

By the time I got to see movies like *Spartacus* and *Marty* which was when I was around 11-12, I also sort of changed my impression of the U.S. Even though we used to get packages from the U.S. from my mother's relatives, like clothes, medicines and toys for me, I had a very bad impression of the U.S., based on government propaganda. Mind you, not from school but from news on the radio and newspapers. Needless to say, my parents did not dare correct my understanding of the U.S. or else they could have disappeared as many had who dared open their mouths.

So this is how other kids and I envisioned Americans:

1) Based on the cartoons we always saw in the newspapers, Americans all had intertwined legs from doing the "twist" - we didn't even know what it meant other than they did not have normal legs
2) They were all part of some "thing" called the KKK, something which we also didn't know anything about other than that they were killing people who didn't agree with them
3) They wanted to destroy us by ruining our crops with an invasion of "Găndaci de Colorado" (Colorado Potato Beetle) which they dropped from planes, like bombs. Bombs of bugs?

But of course, I didn't know what any of this meant. Though questions were always taboo, there was one that finally got to me and that was the "Găndaci de Colorado" attacks since it was in the news a lot, probably because we had a bad year for crops. I asked my mother if her sister, my aunt Joan, was flying planes over our crops and dropping these bugs. Hey – this was a natural question for a small child - she was American and she was the only American I knew of, and here she was trying to starve us by killing our crops. Right?

This time, instead of shushing me away like they always did after dangerous questions, both my parents exploded in hysterics to the point that they had tears in their eyes and of course my question was then repeated to all their friends so everybody had a good time at my expense. Finally I was told that it was not my aunt Joan who was flying the planes but other Americans. Bad, bad American capitalists who wanted to destroy our wonderful socialist country.

How did we get news? All news came from government newspapers and government radio. However, the station that everybody tried to listen to when it wasn't too jammed was Europa Liberă (Radio Free Europe). As I said, by the time I was about 12, I was already much more informed about the real situation in the world, including the truth about the U.S. But when you listened to Radio Free Europe, you had to keep the volume very low, lest a neighbor hear it and report you to the police with the usual consequences for the men of the family. Hmmm, now that I think of it, they never arrested women that I know of. Interesting since there was certainly no sex discrimination; women were forced to work as hard as men when it came to manual labor.

Although the government tried to jam the station, it wasn't quite working to expectations, so rather than risk someone hearing REAL news, as opposed to the propaganda, the government bureaucrats confiscated all the radios from everybody's home and instead installed a gizmo called a "difuzor" which was a wall mounted speaker. As a result we could only listen to one station, the government broadcast.

I must say that other than the ridiculous news that nobody paid attention to, the broadcasts did include hours of classical music which is when I got my first taste of Baroque and Classical music. Of course there was a lot of Tchaikovsky, Stravinsky, Mussorgsky, Shostakovich, Prokofiev and other Russians, as well as our own George Enescu with his superb Romanian Rhapsody and the Ciocârlia (Sky Lark). But there were also tons of Beethoven, Mozart, Bach, Handel, Vivaldi and others, accompanied by captivating details about the composers' lives as well as explanations of the compositions' structure. Despite the despicable and oppressive government, I must say that they did a great job cultivating classical music culture. Of course, this could never include enjoyable Western music like Elvis Presley or Chuck Berry, God forbid.

My aunt Pepi, my father's sister with whom we shared the house, was a very cultivated woman and she also taught me a lot about the lives of the various composers. She was also an avid reader. She just couldn't put a book down, so she took them with her to the outhouse we shared when nature called. Guess it was more pleasant to do your business in an outhouse while reading about the life of Paganini.

I think it's important to clarify that Jews like my aunt and my father who were extremely cultured learned completely on their own from reading books, not from school. At that time, in the 1930s, Jews could not attend classes higher than middle school; therefore nobody went to high school. My mother and her sisters went to Hungarian Catholic schools run by nuns - I always found this amusing.

STELA'S CEMETERY

During the time I lived in Borșa, until 1960, my best friend was Stela Botoș. She was the daughter of the local priest who was my father's good friend. According to my father, he was a very smart and highly educated man - a real intellectual. What a Talmudic scholar like my father had in common with an Orthodox priest is hard to say but there's a saying "great minds think alike" so maybe that's what it was.

One of my favorite after school activities was to go to Stela's house which was near the church with the cemetery behind it. We used to walk around the cemetery and pick flowers and play in it like it was a garden. Actually, it was like being in an outdoor art gallery. Romanian Orthodox cemeteries are beautiful; the headstones are crosses made out of wood and heavily decorated with highly artistic paintings depicting many subjects - sometimes just decorative flowers, sometimes images of the person buried underneath. The most famous Romanian cemetery is the one in Săpânța, known as the Merry Cemetery, which is a popular tourist attraction, much like the tombs in Egypt. Throughout the years, I've found that cemeteries are often fascinating and great places to learn history.

Aside from the sheer beauty of them, we unfortunately lived in an area where wild stories and superstitions about life and afterlife were rampant, especially risings from the grave.

Figure 8 - With my friend Stela

So one day I was in Stela's house and we were chatting in her large living room. I was sitting on the couch in front of a window with a view of the cemetery outside. Also outside near the window was a fabulous lilac tree in full bloom that was gently waving in the wind.

At some point Stela said she was going to the kitchen to get something to drink. While I was waiting quietly on the couch, I heard a gentle knock on the window behind me. I looked behind me at the window - there was nobody there. Then I heard it again, and again I looked and again there was nobody. By then I was getting a little uncomfortable. After all, we were in a cemetery and somebody was knocking on the window and when I looked, it was nobody. Not funny. In fact - scary.

By the fourth knock I literally scrammed out of the room and tripped on the rug between the living room and the next room and there I was – on the floor, out cold! When I came to, Stela and her sisters were hunched over me with some kind of smelling salts or something under my nose and smacking me gently. They didn't understand what happened. I wasn't hurt anywhere because I apparently collapsed gently on the floor, not a hard hit. In other words, I just fainted.

I described the multiple knocks and not seeing anybody, and that I thought it was the ghost of a dead body from the cemetery knocking on the window. After they finished laughing their heads off, they told me it was a branch of the lilac tree that was being blown by the wind and hitting the window.

They didn't want to let me walk home alone so Stela and her sister came with me.

Ok, so my imagination got the best of me and for some time I was the laughing stock of my family. So what else is new?

Arrested at 8

One day, when I was in second grade, around 1955, during a class break that lasted a little longer than usual, 2 of my friends and I climbed up on the roof of the school and removed the national flag. We then paraded around the school yard with the flag as if it were a real holiday parade just the way the communists paraded on the streets during certain holidays. We sang the Romanian and Russian national anthems and all the other kids were amused and followed us so we kept singing these anthems and other national songs as we paraded around the yard.

When one of the teachers came out and saw us, she got very angry and told us to stop and took the flag away. I don't know what happened next, but she must have informed the police because 2 policemen came to the school and arrested us. They took us to the nearby police station.

At that time they were not called the police, but the miliția. The crime we were accused of was an "act against the state" for removing the flag, therefore a political crime, which, had we been adults, would have resulted in our being in jail for about 10 years before a trial even took place.

Fortunately, they really didn't know what to do with us. We were only about 8 years old so they called for our parents. The parents who did show up got a stern lecture about the danger of political acts against the government.

My parents didn't show up – they were terrified of anybody in a military uniform - so the police sent me to the home of a friend of the family who then took me home. I was perplexed and didn't understand the whole thing, but my parents told me not to touch flags anymore. Then they went into their bedroom and giggled like crazy. I still didn't understand what I had done wrong. After all, we marched like good patriotic communists singing our national anthem, just like we saw adults do it on the streets. And I was a Pioneer in good standing. In fact, a year later, I was elected as "Conducătoare de detașament" which I guess translates to "Division Commander" – in all my glory - uniform, Red band around the neck and communist insignia. The honor consisted of walking ahead of my class during a parade. Woohoo!

The beginning of the end

Our life in Romania was beginning to unravel in the mid-fifties as the government became more and more oppressive. The events in the following years are what lead us to escape and settle in the US.

My father in the armoire

My father actually lived in an armoire where he hid for about 7-8 months.

This was around 1955-1956. I call it an armoire because it was really furniture, not built-in closets that are part of modern apartments or houses. This was a really nice armoire, kind of Art Nouveau probably acquired by his uncle in the 1920s when he lived in that house.

As I mentioned, at that time, my father and his twin brother Moisi owned and managed the lumber company named Poposala in Borşa which they got from the Fruchter family. The Fruchter family was very well off and they owned not only the lumber factories but I believe also the gold/silver mines in Baia Borşa.

However, by the time the communist regime started nationalizing everything in 1948, this lumber business was eventually also taken away from us by the government. The nationalization of a business is one thing but these people also nationalized our cow, my father's boots and other "property." I do remember that all these were branded, including the cow and the boots with the insignia "Republica Populară Română".

In any event, since the company was nationalized, my father and his brother were no longer the owners. They were merely employees, even though they were named directors of the company – my uncle was the operations manager and my father was in charge of finance.

At some point, based on a "tip" from one of the employees accusing my father and my uncle of embezzlement, the miliția, arrested my uncle, in the middle of the night, of course, when there was nobody around. My aunt ran over to our house and told my father who immediately ran away to another town. He spent several weeks running from one city to another – Galați, Iași, Bucharest and then finally returned home one night, in the middle of the night and told us that he needed to stay in hiding in the house.

What we had to do was to keep the shades drawn on all the windows, the doors locked and never open them to anybody if we didn't know in advance who it was. The only people who knew that my father was in the house were his sister who lived in the same house as us, his brother's wife and his best friend, Chaim Popovich who was at my parents' wedding.

If someone legitimate knocked at the door like a neighbor or another friend, he would be let in but we first gave my father a signal. That meant that he had to crawl into the bottom drawer of the armoire in their bedroom and stay there until the person left.

This went on for several months until he decided to give himself up because in the interim, they also arrested his brother-in-law, Max Brettschneider, who had nothing to do with the company, as well as his best friend, Chaim Popovici who also had nothing to do with the company.

Obviously, this was a way for the government to force my father to give himself up - which he did.

What was the nature of the embezzlement? The purchase of a heating stove and a typewriter for the office!

After my father was arrested, he spent 8-9 months in jail, without a trial, representation, or anything else remotely resembling justice. During this time, my sister Shari was born, and they allowed my mother to take the baby to the prison in Sighet to show her to my father. My mother took me too but they wouldn't let me in, only my mother and the baby. I usually tease Shari by hinting that she was probably conceived in the armoire.

After about 9 months, an official trial was scheduled although I can't remember exactly where it was held, I do remember being there with my aunt Pepi, my father's sister. Everybody was apprehensive about this trial because the presiding judge was nicknamed the "100-year judge" since he tended to sentence everyone to 100 years, regardless of the nature of the crime.

But on the day of the trial, another judge took over – we knew nothing about him. In retrospect the procedure was totally comical, fantastic and probably completely illegal. It turned out that the prosecutor and the defense attorney were … the same person. He kept moving from one desk to the other to speak. Since I'd never seen a trial before, I found the whole scene bizarre but what did I know? It would have been hilarious, if it hadn't been such a travesty.

In the end, they were all acquitted. And the armoire became a family joke and a source of great amusement to our friends, almost like a tourist attraction.

Meanwhile, there were other ways to hide from the police and we knew of one family that did it in a way that we used to laugh about for years.

This man was my father's friend, Dorian, who used to hang out in the street leaning against a post while smoking a cigarette and watching people pass by. I had no idea why the police were looking for him, and it really didn't matter because they were always looking for someone they deemed "an enemy of the people". It seemed to me that it would have been very simple to arrest him when he was in the street hanging out. Everybody knew him. But no, that would have been too above board and of course everyone could see it.

The miliția liked to arrest people at night by storming their houses. Unfortunately, whenever they stormed into this guy's house, they never found him. And this is why the police were the laughing stock of the town. This man happened to be kind of short and scrawny while his wife Silvia was rather voluptuous and taller than him, in fact she was about twice his size. We later learned that whenever they heard the police at the door, Silvia would get into bed under the covers pretending to be reading, and Dorian would hide under her. When they asked her where her husband was, she always answered that he was at the bodega, all the while she was lying on top of him. We always wondered how he never got crushed because that was one BIG woman. So the police left. It was like a scene from a Laurel and Hardy movie! Really outstanding investigative police work!

Winning (and un-winning) the math prize

One thing that greatly influenced my life and career was the superb education system in Borşa. Communist or not, the school system was so superior and the teachers of such extraordinary skill and knowledge that we all had an intellectual level I never saw in the U.S. when I got here.

As everywhere, some kids learn faster than others but in the end, even those struggling, not only passed all the exams but we used our learned skills in the most amusing ways. For example, we started learning Latin in 4th grade and by the 6th grade we spoke it as fluently as if we were Roman orators. The fact that Romanian is the closest of all the Romance languages to Latin helped a lot, it was almost like learning a dialect. In fact, we used this particular language skill to torment our parents by speaking Latin so they couldn't understand what we were talking about. Of course, planning some goofy escapade, like "Let's go to the movies today" did take some creativity in adapting Latin terms to concepts that didn't exist during Caesar's time. "Movies", was a bit of a challenge, but we did it.

One of my best skills was math – somehow I was just very good in math, and I have to give a lot of credit to my teacher whose name I just can't recall. He was truly extraordinary and influenced my life a lot.

Thanks to his training, I participated in a regional math Olympics (olimpiada) and won first prize which was a trip to Moscow. I was happy that I won but not necessarily enthralled by the nature of the prize. What did I care about Moscow? Thinking back on this event, I realize that no prize would have meant anything to me. I was completely blasé, or maybe I just didn't understand the honor. We did not live in a competitive world so it really didn't mean much to me.

What followed was in a way a validation of my feelings. My father took me by train to …. and here I don't remember to where: Cluj, Sighet, Baia Mare? I don't remember in which city the prize was to be awarded. Maybe I forgot deliberately. Suffice it to say that when we arrived at the building where the prize was to be awarded, there was some commotion and my father explained that instead of the first prize, they gave me the 3rd prize consisting of 4 math books. When I asked why, he said that when they learned that I was Jewish, they had to make the change because they couldn't send a Jew to Moscow.

I remember that on our way back in the train, I was looking through those math books and they were terrific – full of fabulous math tricks which I really enjoyed exploring. As I was smiling at the contents of the books and wanted to show my father one of the formulas, I noticed that he had tears in his eyes. He patted me on the head.

We never spoke about this again.

Shortly after this incident, my father submitted a request to leave the country and all hell broke loose.

THE WRATH AND POWER OF THE POLITICAL PARTY

In 1960 we moved from Borşa to Vişeul de Sus where my father worked as some kind of director at an electrical company named IZA on the Vişeu river.

We were given housing by the company which built 3 houses for its employees right near its headquarters, on the edge of the river. It was an OK house, actually more like a barrack but nobody cared. It had a small entry hall, 2 rooms, a kitchen and a larder. After a few weeks, they threw in another family whom we didn't know but I assumed the husband also worked at the electrical company. As usual, my parents never explained anything, like why there was now another family in one of our rooms. Now, we were 7 people in the house. It was very uncomfortable but there was nothing we could do.

Then, after a few months, disaster - and as usual, our parents never explained to us any details in order to protect us from bad news. Part of the protection was induced by a need for self-preservation — silence was golden. Don't talk!

One day, as I came home from school, I found all our furniture out in the street and my mother crying amid the contents of our house. Turns out we were literally evicted without notice, my father was thrown out of his job and I was thrown out of school.

This was similar to the 1956 math prize event in Borşa but on a different scale. This time, a member of the local Communist party wanted my father's job and he engineered the whole thing because this was the power the party had at that time under Ceausescu. That, coupled with the fact that we applied for an exit visa was the nail in the coffin. We were traitors.

A family who lived up the block from our house took us in and let us use the one finished room in their house under construction. My father got a job at the Jewish Community Center which then found him more permanent lodging in a house that belonged to a rabbi who moved away.

But the rabbi's daughter Ratzele remained in the house.

RATZELE AND THE BRASSIERES

This one took some time to jog my memory – maybe because I just didn't understand what was going on.

When we lived in the rabbi's house, the house and especially the outside backyard smelled of chicken blood and feathers which was really nauseating. This was because the rabbi was also a shochet (ritual slaughterer of poultry) We also shared the house with his daughter who stayed behind after her parents moved away. Her name was Ratzele.

That name alone was comical – a rața (ratza) in Romanian is a duck – so Ratzele was in effect "ducky". That may have been an appropriate name for a little kid, but she was a grown woman, kind of homely, and at age 24 unmarried - in those days, an "old maid".

Her age was also a puzzle – as I mentioned earlier, when I was born and as I grew up, there were only 2 generations of Jews, my parents age and my age and younger – NOTHING in between. So if I was 12 – everybody was either 12 or younger and their parents were my parents' age. There were no grand-parents. I did not see an old Jew until I was about 16, in the US. So for Ratzele to be in her late 20s when I was 12, means she had to have been liberated from a concentration camp at age 15 or 16. I never learned the true story.

The interesting thing about Ratzele was that many people thought she was either a little crazy or a little retarded, or just a little off. She was also an oddity by not fitting into any of the two age groups — so there was a lot of whispering but I could never quite figure out what the problem was. All I know is that she spent her days sewing brassieres and pillow cases. This is all she did all day long– sewing brassieres and pillows. This is also the first time I had seen one of these undergarments, the use of which had never been explained to me by my mother, since she never wore one, and neither did I. In fact no women or girls I knew back then wore brassieres.

Nobody knew why she was sewing brassieres and pillowcases — some people thought that it was the only thing she knew how to make and she had to do something with her time — others suspected that she was preparing her dowry should a suitable husband be found.

We never knew what became of her after we left other than she left the country several years after us.

Expelled from school

My case of being thrown out of school was interesting and certainly ironic. I was in 8th grade at that time. To go from 7th to 8th grade, you had to pass several tests — Romanian, History, Math, Physics, Chemistry, Geography, Biology, Latin, French and a few others. Mind you, I was already in 8th grade which meant that I already passed all those tests.

When my father asked why I was thrown out of school, he was told that I failed one of the tests. And which test was this? Drum roll ...... Math! Wait - how can I have failed a test that I had already passed and with flying colors? I guess anything is possible when the powers that be wanted it that way.

If ever there was a way to figuratively give someone the finger - that was it.

So what do you do when you're 14 and not in school where all the other kids are? We had no television at that time and there were no other outlets for kids so it was really a very bleak situation. My parents decided to get me some kind of private tutoring, and after much research they learned of a French woman who lived in Vişeu who could possibly give me French lessons. My mother set out to find this woman, traipsing through horrible unpaved roads, in the rain and mud and going from house to house to try to find her.

One of the things that puzzled me for many years was why there was a French woman living in Vişeu. There were no foreigners ever, anywhere - certainly not in these remote areas.

In fact the first time I saw an African man was in Borşa around 1958, he was in the back of a truck going up to the mountains. As the truck was hobbling up the rural unpaved roads, there were dozens of children running after the trucks trying to get a closer glimpse of that young man. The truck finally stopped and the young man got out and it was extraordinary to see these kids touching him everywhere, looking at his hands, the color of the skin on his palms, everything. They were like little children checking out a new toy. The young man was very charming, he must have been going through this a lot, and explained in perfect Romanian that he was a medical student from Ghana studying at the University in Cluj, and he was going to the tuberculosis sanatorium that was up in the Prislop mountains.

So why was a French woman living in Viseu, in a neighborhood called Ziptzerai which was known to be an area inhabited by a small German and Hungarian population? No idea.

My mother finally found this woman and she became my tutor forcing me to learn conversational French very quickly because she did not speak Romanian and I had no other way of communicating with her.

During this private training, my father was approached by the principal of the school who told him that there was a way to get me back in school. The path was a weekly poker game with the school principal, the mayor of the town and the man who took over my father's job.

The mechanics of the poker game were that my father would lose every session so that the money could go "legally" to the winners. Since we had no money, the Jewish community collected money to give to my father so he could lose it at the weekly poker game.

After a few games, we were informed by the central government in Bucharest that we were approved to leave the country so my father made various excuses to interrupt the weekly game until we hightailed it out of there in the middle of the night. In other words, he never told his poker "partners" about our impending departure. Obviously, they didn't know. The notification didn't go through the regional channels, it came directly from Bucharest.

So how did we get the papers to leave? My mother's family in New York, working through H.I.A.S., the Hebrew Immigrant Aid Society, found a Romanian man in São Paulo, Brazil, who submitted an application to the Romanian government, along with a payment of $5,000 to let my father out so he could come to work in his factory in São Paulo because my father was supposedly the only person who could perform some specific job in his factory.

What that factory was or what the job was, nobody knew or cared. Obviously, the $5,000 was all they wanted as long as there was no mention of Israel or America. These two countries were taboo in 1962 at the height of the Cold War but Israel became acceptable several years later when the rest of my father's family and other Jews were allowed to emigrate to Israel.

So we said good bye to Communist Romania which was also a bittersweet revenge for us. We learned that 2 weeks after we left, the police came looking for my father again. Obviously they didn't know we had left the country - the usual right hand/ left hand incompetence typical of most bureaucracies.

Leaving Romania

THE FIRST TIME I EVER flew on a plane was when we left Romania in the summer of 1962 for our new life, supposedly in São Paulo, Brazil.

It didn't start off well, but considering that we were so used to being abused, I shouldn't have been surprised at what happened. Before we got on the plane, we were asked to strip naked (must have been shades of things past for my mother from when she was in Auschwitz), an act which I found perfectly normal. Mind you, they were not looking for bombs or anything illegal. Given the notorious corruption of Communist governments, they were simply looking for anything they could steal from us before we left the country. And this didn't happen only to us; we learned that Jews who left Poland and other Communist countries at that time experienced the same outrage.

This reinforced the widely held notion that Romanians were thieves you know: the standard Borscht Belt joke in the Catskills:

Question: *How do you make Romanian chicken soup?*
Answer: *First, you steal your neighbor's chicken.*

Despite this established cultural misconception, we were open to any kind of abuse so it's easy to understand why nobody resisted when they confiscated valuables such as my father's wallet, my necklace, my mother's few pieces of jewelry, and even removed my 5 year old sister's tiny little earrings from her pierced ears.

What kind of documents did we have for boarding a plane to a foreign country?

Certainly not passports. They were named Certificat de Călătorie (Travel Certificate), 2 page documents that indicated the 2 countries we were allowed to pass through on the way to Brazil. and they were more like bills of lading, like when you ship products. Or like an invoice, the only difference was there was no price attached to any of our names.

The papers also stipulated that we had no citizenship so that wherever we landed we would probably be detained for a certain amount of time while asking for asylum. But at this point we couldn't care less but would have been more at ease had we known the role HIAS would be playing in resettling refugees like us. But, then we also had never heard of HIAS before this trip.

First Interpreter Job on Tarom Airline

Finally, we were now aboard a Tarom Airline flight. About 45 minutes into the flight, there was a big commotion at the front of the plane. Since we had no experience flying or of any dangers associated with planes, like crashes, we did not pay too much attention. That is until they announced on the speakers that they were looking for somebody who spoke French. At this point, my mother, who never pushed me into anything, raised my hand and screamed "My daughter speaks French". I was mortified. Not only was I not used to being "promoted" by my mother, but here I was scared to death on this flying coffin and my mother was offering me up as a sacrifice in mid-air? I was simply terrified of being on the plane.

They asked me to come to the front and explained to me that one of the French passengers was having a fit and they couldn't speak to him because he didn't speak Romanian.

Just to clarify, at this time, in the early 1960s, the French auto manufacturer Renault was building cars in the eastern region of Romania. I believe that this was when the Dacia car first appeared. Until then, the only cars one ever saw were the Russian Volgas. Therefore, there were many French Renault employees going back and forth to Romania and on this flight a group of French engineers was flying home on vacation. Of course they were, after all it was August when all of France is closed for vacation. Sorry about that, I just couldn't resist the little jab.

One particular man was apparently having some kind of nervous breakdown because he kept insisting that he wanted to get off the plane - in mid-flight, of course. I finally translated to him that he could get off in about ½ hour when the plane landed in Vienna and then do whatever he wanted to. He thanked me, asked for an aspirin and sat down. That's when I first found out that the plane was stopping in Vienna. I thought we were going to Brazil. But that's another story.

LANDING IN VIENNA

The stop in Vienna was known by all those involved in our extrication from Romania except for us. One of the reasons was that it was very difficult to communicate. Telephone conversations were monitored – yes even then – and letters and packages were opened. One year, my mother's family in New York sent us some winter clothes including boots. The boots came with their soles ripped open, and therefore unwearable. They were checking to see if dollar bills were hidden inside the shoe soles.

Since every letter we got from America arrived opened, my parents and mom's family in New York used various codes to communicate. I don't remember all of them but for example, talking about dollars was referred to as Penicillin and the dollar amounts in milligrams or some other measurement.

The surprise landing in Vienna was not at all perplexing since we were used to being kept in the dark about any plans, including travel plans. Well, it was mainly my parents who were used to being carted away without any questions asked lest you risk some kind of abuse. Being the frightened sheep that we were trained to be about ever asking questions, nobody asked why we were landing in Vienna. Maybe the other passengers knew but we didn't. We acted like and were basically treated like cattle.

It soon became apparent what the plan was when they called my father's name and told him we had to get off the plane. Of course, he never asked why. He just told us we had to get off the plane. So we did.

As we got off the plane, two men approached us on the tarmac and said they were friends of my uncle Eddie, my mother's brother, from New York and the family sent them here to pick us up as we would be staying in Vienna for a while to wait for a visa to the US. That was the first time we learned that we were not going São Paulo in Brazil, but to the US. That was some shocker, but I guess a good one for my mother as she was going to finally be reunited with her family. Frankly, I was kind of disappointed that I wouldn't be seeing any monkeys in the Brazilian jungle, an experience I was really looking forward to.

They drove us to an apartment building where a distant aunt named Ghitu lived and whom I'd never met before. Needless to say, the whole thing was very strange but we just followed instructions. We were to stay with her until the HIAS found us a more permanent apartment.

The next day, the two gentlemen from the airport picked us up and drove us to visit the former Mauthausen concentration camp.

Having never been in a car before, and sitting in the back seat for over an hour drive, I was so car sick that I threw up on my sister's shoes and by the time we got to that camp, I just sat outside the car trying not to puke again in front of everybody. I think the reason we went there was because it was the first concentration camp built by the Germans in Austria after its annexation in 1938 and they wanted us to see it. Besides the carsick episode, all I remember about that visit is the section of the building that was filled with a mountain of children's shoes – the shoes of children that were killed there. It was really horrible. This was certainly not the first thing I needed to see in the free world. If you visit the Holocaust museum in Washington DC, you will see a mountain of shoes there too. Nothing makes the experience more real and horrifying than imagining who wore these shoes and what became of them.

After that visit, they took us to a pastry shop where we had coffee and cakes. This is when my father told Shari that now he could answer any question in the world she had, that now he could speak freely since we were in a free country.

The first apartment we lived in with my aunt in Vienna was right near the Stefansdom Cathedral, on Bauernmarkt and across the street from a nightclub called the Flamingo. This nightclub was a learning experience for me because I used to see these beautiful women walking in all the time, in striking clothes and sparkling jewelry and in particular something I had not seen before -- an ankle bracelet. So I asked my aunt what this place was with these beautiful and elegant women and the ankle bracelets. She explained that it was a night club – being the country bumpkin from Transylvania, I of course didn't know what a nightclub was so she explained. But when I asked about the ankle bracelet, she shoved me over to my father and whispered something in his ear. My father cracked up and took me aside and said that it was ladies who were paid to dance with men. It was his way of explaining they were hookers and apparently the ankle bracelet was the signature. Sounded strange but hey, I was in a new world, who knew what else was to come?

After several weeks, the HIAS found us another apartment which we shared with another refugee family. This apartment was on Gentzgasse, not far from the Volksoper. The apartment we shared with the other family was gigantic. At least our two rooms were huge. Unfortunately, one of the rooms, which was designated as the bedroom, had only one bed, a large bed but just one, for a family of four. After about 2 weeks, they brought another small bed, for me.

But until my bed came, the four of us slept in one bed, which was against the wall. It was very tight. My father was at the edge, my mother next to him, then me and Shari against the wall. Because it was so tight, we all had to sleep on one side, the same side, so we didn't breathe into each other's faces. In the middle of the night, my father would wake up, and command: *Achtung! Umdrehen!* (Attention! Turn around). So we would all turn to the other side. My father had a great sense of humor, we were hysterical!

During the 7-8 months we were in Vienna I never went to school. The local high schools would not accept me because I couldn't speak German; the French school threw me out for some infraction that I don't remember; the American school did accept me but by then I just didn't want to go to school anymore. I knew we were in transit so what was the point? My parents didn't object.

So for 7 months, instead of going to school, I played poker with the other refugee kids, drank dark beer and sausage for 1.80 schillings and went to the opera every day. They let kids in for free. The Volksoper was a little lower level than the grand opera so it was more Johann Strauss rather than Mozart. But it was a good way to pass the time. I think I saw the *Merry Widow* six times.

Welcome to New York

We did not go directly to New York from Vienna. We were first taken to Rome where we spent about 2 weeks waiting for some documents. I don't remember the place in Rome that well. It was kind of a ghetto where all of us refugees stayed while we were waiting to go to New York.

During that time, I remember going shopping with my mother for some groceries and the lady behind the counter, hearing us speak Romanian, asked us what part of Italy were we from. I suppose Romanian sounded like some Southern Italian dialect. When we told her we were from Romania, she was shocked. She had never met a Romanian and didn't know the language was so close to Italian. I'm glad we had an opportunity to entertain some Italians during our short stay in Rome.

We arrived in at Idlewild Airport (now JFK) on Alitalia Airlines on February 7, 1963. This was an auspicious date since 4 days later was my 16th birthday. Sweet Sixteen?

My mother's family picked us up at the airport and it was a momentous occasion. They drove us to the apartment they rented for us in Flushing, Queens which was completely furnished with a refrigerator full of food and drinks. We even had a telephone: OL(ympia)7-0755. I can't believe the amount of time, energy and money they put into getting us out of Romania and to the U.S. We were really bewildered.

After barely 3 days in the country, my mother's family, 3 brothers and 3 sisters, told us that the family would celebrate my birthday because every girl in the US had a Sweet Sixteen Party. It was also my cousin Harvey's birthday; he is 3 years younger than I. Harvey's mother, my aunt Loretta, was to pick us up and drive us to her house for the party and the rest of the family would be meeting us there.

My aunt showed up with her daughter Ronnie and we all got into the car. I sat in the back with my father, Shari and Ronnie. My mother sat in the front with my aunt.

I remember that my aunt got upset because she was trying to make a left turn at an intersection on Union Turnpike but was forced to go straight ahead because there was a No Left Turn sign. This took her to a road she didn't know. I believe it was the Interboro Parkway, now the Jackie Robinson Parkway, and I remember her getting upset because she was lost and she had a roast in the oven that would burn if she didn't get home on time. That's the last thing I remember other than a light pole coming up on the left side of the road.

The next thing I knew was that I woke up in a hospital and a doctor was asking me in French how I was feeling. It was Booth Memorial Hospital, now part of New York Hospital.

What happened, based on what I have been told, is that my aunt crashed into the light pole. The 2 people most badly injured were my mother who went through the windshield and me, hitting my head on the right side rear window. My father, Shari and Ronnie were OK.

My mother was in the hospital for about 4 weeks and required cosmetic plastic surgery which was not at its best in 1963. Her slashed lip scar is still visible.

I was apparently in a coma for 3 days and when I woke up I could only speak French. I could have spoken Romanian, Hungarian, German or French – so why just French? Who knows? The mysteries of the brain are indeed mysterious.

The hospital assigned a French speaking doctor, Dr. Matei Roussan, to communicate with me and translate for my father. I was released after 5 days when the Romanian language returned to me.

That was our Welcome to America experience and my Sweet Sixteen rolled into one.

Early Academic Disappointments

As I mentioned, I was born in Sighet, but grew up in Borşa, a small village in Transylvania, in the county of Maramureş, the northern-most province of Romania.

The name, Transylvania alone used to send people in the U.S. into retreat – at least in the early 1960's when I first set foot here. Whenever I was asked where I was from, due to my accent of course, I decided to say Transylvania because at that time, nothing else worked. Most people I met in New York did not know where Romania was, or even what it was. Then I thought I'd say Austria as we lived there before coming to the US and it was at least a West European country and since at that time I spoke fluent German and could pass for Austrian, I assumed that people would at least be able to place me more or less geographically. Wrong. That didn't work either, the usual response was, "All the way from Australia?" Oy! I was not alone in this geographic miasma; my best friend Daisy who also came from Austria several years before me, had the same experience. Whenever she said she was from Austria, the next questions were about kangaroos.

So I decided to stick with Transylvania because I was always amused by the instant sense of recognition – not geographic, but Hollywood training, so the reaction was usually bug-eyes, followed sometimes by a furtive look at my teeth. So what – I love to be amused and if I could make someone's day by making them believe they met some kind of mythical monster, why not? Probably made for good conversation at home during dinner, "I met this vampire girl from Transylvania …."

I must admit that this was not at the Harvard Club or some other elite location, but in Flushing, Queens, so maybe the intellectual level was somewhat more limited in that area at the time. Unfortunately, I didn't fare any better in Manhattan. The utter ignorance of geography was quite unsettling. I realized that whenever I took a taxi. At that time, most taxi drivers were local New Yorkers and without fail, the first question after I gave the destination, was "You have an accent - where you from?" Not "where are you from?" I was beginning to learn New York English – get rid of superfluous verbs.

After a while trying to explain the geographical and then political situation in Romania, I decided that I needed a response that would shorten the conversations somewhat. Though all taxi drivers, except one (but more about that later) could not have been more pleasant, I wasn't always in the mood for chatter and didn't want to appear rude, so I developed a new background which I thought would shorten the conversation. Therefore my response was something like "I am actually from Kentucky but since my family was in the army, I'm an army brat and I lived in various countries and that's why I have an accent." The question that inevitably followed was: "Oh, your father is in army?" Answer: "No, it's my mother, she's a colonel in the army, my father just tags along." That kind of ended the conversation.

Jamaica High School

The reason I mention my enrollment in high school in February 1963, just two weeks after my "welcome to the USA coma" is to compare the education in Romania with what I had to look forward to in America.

My aunt Joan came with me to meet the principal, Louis Schuker, because I couldn't speak a word of English and someone had to translate.

Given that my English language skills were so non-existent, Mr. Shuker said that I was to be enrolled in a freshman class, in other words, with students 2 years younger than I. If you've ever been 16, you know how offensive it is for a teenager – even an immigrant like me – to be forced to hang out with younger kids.

My aunt vehemently protested the unfairness of placing me with kids at a lower level of education than I had. When my aunt translated to me what she said, I got really enraged – I think that having gone through many indignities as a child, having been out of school for almost 2 years, coming out of a coma from a horrible accident, I kind of grew some cojones (yes, figurative) that made me combative like I'd never been before.

I think that by then, I just really didn't care about anything anymore and now being in a so-called free country, (though I really didn't even know what that meant) I threw a temper tantrum and screamed that if my language skills were to be the defining factor for my grade placement, I should really be placed in kindergarten since 5-year olds speak English better than I did.

The principal, who knew my aunt, was amused by my outburst and suggested that I take a test in various subjects to see what my general level was – excluding English, of course.

I thought that was a good idea. So after losing a year of high school in Romania (when I was thrown out of school) and another 6 months in Vienna where I spent my time drinking beer and playing poker every night, what do you think my education level scored?

2 years of college!

I was therefore placed in a junior (3rd year) class where I rightfully belonged and despite my bad English, I actually tutored the kids in my class to pass the math tests. The class average in math at that time in mid-year was 45, in other words, a solid F. By the end of the year, everybody passed and some even got Bs and As.

I must say that the principal was a really nice person and very dedicated to academic excellence but unfortunately he was trapped in a decaying educational system. The math teacher who was assigned to my class was an idiot. I wanted to ask math-related questions in class, but since I couldn't speak English, I asked my French teacher, in French of course, if she could translate my question to the teacher. She did, and his answer was, "It's hard to say". It was a question about trigonometry put to a math teacher. Enough said?

So much for the education system in US. It didn't make me feel too secure, a sentiment that was reinforced over and over again by people I met over the years – not at all stupid or lacking in intellect, just a lack of some of the basics of education which was not their fault. It was and still is the shortcomings of the system.

That semester I failed English and Social Studies because I didn't understand a word of what was going on in the class. Of course I passed Math and French, but French barely because I couldn't translate exercises into English or vice-versa. I felt as though I were on another planet. I went to summer school and watched a lot of soap operas and by the end of August I spoke English fluently. There's nothing like immersion in TV to pick up a language quickly

In my senior year, since I was so far ahead of everybody educationally, there were not many courses for me to take where I would actually learn something so I took basket weaving and typing and some other classes that I never considered to be part of an education system. It was most depressing and stressful to be in such an environment, and as a result I developed stomach ulcers and had to start drinking coffee with milk and other drab foods. No more *dunkel bier und wurst zu eins achtzig!*

"Prostitutes" in Jamaica High School
Now this is a typical country bumpkin episode.

As I said before, our first apartment in Vienna was across the street from the Flamingo nightclub, and that that was the first time I had ever seen hookers and the ankle bracelet symbolic of Viennese "hookery".

Imagine my surprise when I arrived at Jamaica High School several months later and noticed that half the girls in the school were wearing ankle bracelets!

I remember coming home one day and screaming at my parents that I didn't want to go to school anymore because it was full of hookers! My parents were very upset because they didn't know what to do about it and were wringing their hands in dismay and helplessness. They were also uncomfortable about asking the family why there are so many hookers in a high school. I mean, hookers were just not part of the society we grew up in so it was not a well-known "profession", at least not for bumpkins from Transylvania. Of course they never asked me what made me think all these girls were hookers. They thought it might have been some American tradition that we were not familiar with and were just too embarrassed to ask for an explanation.

After they made some subtle inquiries with the family, I was set straight by my cousin Bob who explained the concept of going steady (in 1963) and some dating protocols. In other words, girls who had a steady boyfriend wore ankle bracelets. Kind of like the concept of an engagement ring. Duh!

Other Social Fails

During my first days in high school, although all the students in my classes were very nice to me, it was difficult for them to communicate with me. The only person who spoke to me outside of class, like in the lunch room, was a girl named Susan Abramowitz. I think she just took pity on me because she saw how lost I was, not speaking English and kind of frightened to the point that during written tests, I even misspelled my name on top of the sheet. Of course, I always handed in blank pages, I had no idea what the teacher was talking about, in English and Social Studies, the two courses I failed that first semester. I remember the Social Studies teacher looking at my paper and saying with pity in his eyes, "Renee, you misspelled your name". Of course I didn't understand what he said and the other kids in class just looked away, probably embarrassed and feeling sorry for me.

Susan somehow decided to follow me around, I guess she was afraid I'd fall out of some window, or down the toilet. She spent a lot of time with me in the lunch room trying to talk to me, helping me pick the food in the line and just generally being very kind, attentive and instructional. After a few weeks, I was able to mumble a bit in English, and even understand some jokes.

So one day, while we were sitting in the lunch room, a boy came over and bent down over me asking me what I was doing Saturday night. I was a little surprised at this question so I answered, "I don't know yet. It's only Tuesday".

At which point Susan kicked me under the table, and whispered "He's asking you out". HUH? So I said that I think I'll be babysitting Saturday night. This generated another kick under the table with a "Don't say that." whisper.

At this point, the poor guy left realizing I was a lost cause. Susan explained that he was asking me out on a date to go to the movies. This followed by an explanation of what a "date" was and that you never mention babysitting because that implies that you are not popular and therefore have no dates on the weekend.

She also explained the honor of being asked out for a Saturday night date as opposed to a Friday night date, which was considered less desirable. Oh yes, I really thought I was on another planet.

Then, she proceeded to explain the concept of a curfew, which I also failed when another girl once asked me what my curfew was when she invited me to a party.

Susan then explained that when a boy asks me for my curfew, I shouldn't say "What?" I have to say 11:00 or 11:30PM, because that means my parents expected me to be back at that time. If I didn't have a curfew, it meant that I was a slut. My parents? Ha! They had no such conception. If I came home at 4AM, the first thing my mother would ask was whether I was hungry.

That was just too much information for me, what with the ankle bracelets fiasco, and these dating rules, I told her that these rituals were just too complicated for me while I was thinking that I wanted to go back to Vienna and play poker and drink beer.

But by the end of the summer, after I went to summer school to repeat the two classes I failed, I spoke English quite fluently and I was ready for a date. My acquired proficiency in English came from watching soap operas and American Bandstand. Dick Clark had a very clear enunciation.

My first date was Freddy Morales. I believe the date was arranged by my friend and neighbor Daisy who was "dating" his older brother Bob. We went to the movies. He asked me if he was my first date since I came to the US. Of course he was, but by then I had learned the tips and tricks of dating and I didn't want to appear as though I had just gotten off the boat, so I lied, "Oh no, I had a few dates with Romanian boys but you are the first American".

Not bad, eh? Yes, I'm a fast learner! Sorry Freddy, I do apologize, I lied - you were my first date in the U.S.

Unfortunately, every time I had an unpleasant experience that I felt was above my ability to control or deal with, I wanted to go back to Vienna where I had such a good time.

This time it was a tragedy that scared the daylights out of me. I almost felt it was safer to go back to Romania where you could go to jail, but not this. What was this? The assassination of President Kennedy!

I was horrified, crestfallen, scared but mostly disillusioned that something horrific like this could happen in what I assumed was the most civilized country in the world. Yes, I knew about Lincoln but that was in the past, just like all the assassinations we learned about in history classes.

I thought we were past that kind of savagery. Though I didn't know anything about politics I got used to seeing this charming President Kennedy, his lovely wife and cute children. It was almost like a distant family. I'd never seen this before. When I was in Romania, I didn't even know that Ceasusescu had a wife or a family. We never knew anything about anybody unless something appeared in a newspaper, government newspaper of course, or heard on the state radio. The only time we saw him was a picture in a newspaper at a podium making a speech.

But having been in the country by now for about 8 months, I began to feel connected not only to the country but the leadership. I think television had much to do with it – it was real human beings as opposed to a black and white picture in a newspaper. The President of the United States was a real human being, almost like a touchable figure. So this horrible tragedy affected me to the point of again wanting to go back to Vienna where at least even though we lived in a bit of a fog, it was a peaceful fog, not one filled with horrors.

ADELPHI UNIVERSITY

After I graduated from high school, I applied to several colleges but the one I really wanted to go to was Queens College because it was free.

Unfortunately, even though I did quite well in the SATs even in English, my grades from high school were not up to the standard of Queens College, where at the time, you needed a minimum of a B+ average. I guess my basket weaving and typing classes in my senior year in high school didn't do much to raise my average. It was obvious that these two acquired skills were not going to be a factor in my career. Therefore I applied to several other colleges in the area and I was accepted at Adelphi University.

The tuition at Adelphi University was quite high and of course, no scholarship since my high school grades were below the benchmark. And since it was in Garden City, it was very inconvenient to get to from Flushing, especially without a car.

It was also the perfectly wrong college for someone like me at that time. Not that there was anything wrong with the university itself, it was just way out of my league, not academically but socially and financially. Here I was this "green" immigrant who lived in Queens going to a school where most of the students came from the Five-Towns, a group of high income neighborhoods in Nassau County. Of course at the time I didn't know what that was, but I did notice that they used to come to school in a variety of different cars, the girls had fancy jewelry and during Winter and Spring vacations, they went to Rome or Paris.

But there were two benefits: I got to see the Beach Boys in person performing at the school auditorium and I had a date with a boy named Billy who drove a Racing Green Jaguar XKE. I fell in love. With the car of course, not Billy.

Since I still yearned for Queens College, I decided to transfer to Queens College for night classes. I was hoping that going to night school there would bring up my grades to permit me to transfer to day classes. That is exactly what happened, and by the time I was a junior, I was in day school.

Queens College

By the time I was a senior, I was getting restless. Since I was majoring in French Literature, I found out that the college had a one year study abroad program in France and I jumped at the opportunity. France, here I come! Besides the restlessness, there was another reason, a bit more lame but not so unusual for a young girl. I had a boyfriend who was drafted into the army during the Vietnam war. He got lucky and instead of Vietnam was stationed in Stuttgart, Germany, which is not too far from France. Unfortunately the relationship didn't work out.

Since I spent my senior year abroad, as opposed to the typical junior year abroad, the end of the year meant that I would graduate with a Bachelor of Arts degree. Not so fast – regardless of how I was going to do in my senior year in France, I received a letter from Queens College while I was in France that I was in danger of not graduating because I had failed ... Tennis! The problem was that my grades weren't that good, mainly due to my failings in high school and to be honest, I didn't find the classes very stimulating.

Maybe that's why I wanted to go away to France, or maybe it was something else, I don't know. I just know I was antsy and really had no vision of a future after I graduated. I still felt that I didn't fit in socially or academically. It was also the height of the Vietnam war which I really didn't understand that well. I knew it was about fighting Communism but it seemed like such a waste and I just wasn't used to seeing young men drafted into the army to go and fight in some distant land. The whole thing was off my radar.

There is only one thing that made my last year at Queens College enjoyable and that was my social life. I met some students who became my friends for life. There were also a number of Iranian students who were there on a scholarship from the Iranian government at the time of the Shah of Iran. These guys were the wildest bunch of guys I ever met. They were definitely more into partying than studying – I'm not sure how many of them even graduated. They loved expensive clothes like $200 shoes which at that time was a fortune, silk shirts and fancy cars. One of them was the son of the UN Ambassador from Iran so with a UN license plate you could do anything mere mortals couldn't; like park anywhere, speed, and generally behave like wild children - with no consequences.

They also favored popular restaurants and clubs which I'd never heard of, and one such place was Max's Kansas City which was on Park Avenue South. At that time, Max's had a restaurant on the main floor and a club on the upper floor so it was not yet the wild punk rock club it became later. This is also when I met the girlfriend of one of these guys, Norma Kamali, who had married one of the two Kamali brothers who were in class with me.

I remember one evening when we were having dinner there with my bunch of friends, we were sitting at a long table with some other people I didn't know. We all introduced each other and one couple was Mike Nichols and Elaine May, another Betty Comden and Adolph Green. Needless to say, we had no clue who they were so we just said "nice to meet you" and continued with our steaks.

Obviously, Broadway was not in our universe at that time.

By June 1968, just as I was preparing for my trip to France, another horrible event took place so I felt it was really my destiny to get away from here as fast as possible. It was the assassination of Bobby Kennedy. There are no words to describe my state of mind other than, Run! And run I did, well, not literally but sailing across the ocean to France.

Wacky Trips

But before we get to my trip to France, I realize that one thing that seemed to color all my trips after I left Romania was some level of absurdity, comedy, fright or downright danger due mainly to the fact that I never planned ahead. But then that's a characteristic of youth – adventure. Stupidity was another characteristic, at least in my case. But then there are always unforeseen catastrophes that are nobody's fault.

Here are some examples.

Israel – week after the 6 Day War 1967

In the Spring of 1967, my parents went to Israel to visit my father's family whom they hadn't seen since we left Romania. This family consisted of my father's twin brother and sister who left Romania a couple of years after us and emigrated to Israel. There was also a sister who left for Israel around 1947, meaning that my father hadn't seen her in over 20 years.

Because my parents had a great time I decided to go too during my summer vacation I arrived in Tel-Aviv in the middle of June, 1967, about a week after the Six-Day war. Needless to say, had I known there was going to be a war, I would have never made the trip. But since I bought the tickets 2 months before, and nobody warned me that there was going to be a war, I landed one week after the war ended. That means I was surrounded by military with guns everywhere, especially in all public places. It was a bit disconcerting, sort of bringing back memories of another era when we were surrounded by guns.

Of course I stayed with various family members and since they were spread between Tel-Aviv and Haifa, I got to see a lot of interesting places.

After the obligatory trip to Jerusalem, I contacted a girl I met on the plane trip over and asked her if she wanted to come with me to Eilat. That was kind of a long trip and I didn't want to go alone. I remember her name was Shoshana. We agreed to meet at the central bus station and after we went to the Dead Sea and then through the desert to visit other attractions, we were to continue to Eilat. We planned to stop at a hostel outside Eilat since it was much cheaper than a hotel.

Just as a reminder to anyone who has been to Israel recently, it is important to keep in mind that this was in 1967 — 40+ years ago when the country was nowhere near as developed as it is now.

First there was the central bus station in Tel-Aviv, the Tahana Merkazit. I had nightmares about it for years. Even though I came from a primitive country where all sorts of livestock were roaming in the streets, I was not prepared to see all these critters on a bus. The entire area was mayhem: busses, people, goats, chickens, and soldiers. Except for the busses, the place looked like some medieval Middle Eastern market place. When we got on our bus, we were sitting behind two Arabs with a chicken, a duck and a goat. The goat kept nibbling at my skirt. Behind us was another zoo and all the way in the back were a bunch of Hassidic Jews. It was the oddest bus ride I ever took.

We finally got to our destination, the hostel, and promptly went to take a nap so that we could be ready in the early evening for our trek to Eilat. This hostel was in the middle of nowhere, so there was nothing to be seen besides the main road and some hills on both sides of the road.

We asked the manager which was the best way to go to Eilat and he said that we could either take a taxi, which he would have to call for since there was nothing around the hostel. Or wait for the bus until the next day. Or we could walk – it was only about 1 ½ miles and then perhaps take a taxi back.

That sounded OK to us so we set out on the road to Eilat. As we walked and yacked like two typical young girls, the sun started setting on the west so the hills on the right side of the road started to glimmer in the setting sun. Looking back now, I wish we had had a camera because seeing Bedouins on camels on the crest of the hill in the setting sun was something out of a painting. It was breathtaking.

We kept walking and yakking and by now it had gotten a lot darker but we felt OK, there was also no traffic after a while which was kind of odd but we didn't think much of it. It was really fun to be walking on a road in dead silence around us.

And then, out of nowhere, without a sound, as if materializing out of thin air, we found ourselves with two rifles in our faces and being yelled at in some language by two soldiers with four other ones behind them, all with their guns drawn. At that point we simply froze and I whispered to Shoshana "Oh shit".

Then I heard one of the soldiers in the back saying something that I didn't understand but I heard the word "American". All of this took about 20 seconds. They lowered the firearms and one soldier came forward and asked as if we were American. We said yes.

He then asked us what we were doing on this road. We replied that we were walking to Eilat because we were told it was not far from our hostel.

At this point he smiled and said, "Do you know where this road is going?" He didn't wait for our answer and said, "This is the road to Aqaba – you are walking to Jordan. You took the wrong turn at the fork a while back. We have been watching you since then."

Needless to say, we did not notice any fork in the road but by then we were so rattled that we could not speak, just stood there like some dummies, then burst out crying. The soldiers said they would drive us back to the hostel in their Jeep or whatever that vehicle was. During the drive, we asked them if we should try to visit Sharm-el-Sheik since it had been seized by Israel during the war the week before. They agreed that with our sense of direction, we would probably end up in Egypt at which point they would no longer be able to save us.

They suggested we go back to Tel Aviv and avoid any more border areas. I think he wanted to say that we were too stupid to get around in this kind of war zone so we should keep to safe areas. Because we were morons. He didn't say that, but I'm sure he was thinking it. So we never got to see Eilat.

The next morning, we had one of those hardy Israeli breakfasts with all sorts of exotic salads and other delicacies and then got back on the bus to Tel-Aviv. But before we left, the manager told us to make a stop in Be'er Sheva because it was Thursday which is market day and it could be fun.

So we did stop and it really was fun – all the merchants were Bedouins and they were hawking all sorts of hand made products and livestock.

We bought some jewelry but the most fun I had was when one of the merchants came over to me and asked me something I did not understand. He was pointing to Shoshana so I thought he was asking her name so I told him that her name was Shoshana. Another merchant, who overheard the conversation, came to me and clarified in English that the man was offering me two goats in exchange for Shoshana.

Needless to say, I did not get it. I asked him exactly what he was saying because I didn't understand what that meant. The man who spoke English finally explained that I was being offered two goats if the man could keep Shoshana to marry her because she was a blonde.

Holding my breath so I didn't explode laughing, I replied that Shoshana did not belong to me so he had to ask her directly if she wanted to stay here and marry him and I would be happy to accept the 2 goats. Shoshana gave me a look like she was going to kill me and I had to turn away so she couldn't see me holding back my hysteria. I think she thanked him for the kind offer but said that she had she had to go back to school and would come back when school was over.

The ride back to Tel-Aviv was a non-stop torture session for Shoshana - I was relentless in accusing her of ruining me financially by depriving me of the goats and had she allowed me negotiate a bit, I could probably had obtained a camel too. This went on until we got back on the plane to NY and continued for several months with our friends. To our friends we were the laughing stock of the summer of 1967. But seriously, the goats were so cute!

FRANCE 1968-1969

Another foreign trip was the 1968-69 school year I spent in France as part of the Queens College Study Abroad Program. Originally, we were supposed to be at the university in Reims which I was really looking forward to since it's in the middle of champagne country. I was dreaming about champagne orgies, bathing in champagne – driving around the countryside and hopping from vineyard to vineyard. Notice I wasn't thinking much about studying which was the purpose of the whole trip.

Unfortunately, due to the student revolution of 1968 which ended with the toppling of the de Gaulle government, the Reims university campus was closed and as a result, we went instead to the Université de Nancy, in Lorraine.

The trip to France was on a student ship, although at the time I didn't know exactly what a student ship was as opposed to a regular ship. Having been on other ships years later, I assume it was a student ship because every cabin contained 4 bunk beds and no luxury accommodations. The ship held some 2,000 students plus I guess a number of teachers. Anyway, the name of the ship was the S. S. Aurelia.

The itinerary was that we would first cross the Atlantic to someplace in England and then across the Channel to Calais and from there proceed by train to Nancy. One hour after we left New York harbor, we were served dinner. The soup was dancing in the plate. Bread rolls were rolling on the floor. I got kind of dizzy and told my friends that I was going back to the cabin. That was the last time I saw the dining room until we were on the English Channel, about 5 days later.

I was sick, confined to my bunk for the entire trip, until we got to Southampton. I was weak from a lack of food for a week because all I had was a banana and a roll which my cabin-mates brought me once a day. But by the sixth day, I was finally able to climb down from my upper level bunk because the ship didn't seem to rock as much. I was taken to the top-deck which I learned is the best place to be when you're seasick.

On the way to Calais, I had my first meal in a week. This trip cured me of ever wanting to go on a cruise. In fact, just looking at a boat on the water makes me seasick.

NANCY - FRANCE
The trip to Nancy was fine except that when we arrived we were all eagerly waiting for our trunks. All of us travelled with a trunk since we were going to be away for a year. When my trunk arrived, surprise! I didn't have to even

look at the name. I knew it was not mine because it came with a pair of skis tied to the top of the trunk.

Of course it was not my trunk, but some other student's whose last name was also Schneider. He was going to Aix-en-Provence. I guess he was planning to go skiing during Christmas vacation - definitely a good idea. Therefore his trunk was in Nancy and mine was in Aix. After a few frantic phone calls between our 2 universities, the trunks were finally shipped to the correct owners. We were all curious about what was in this guy's trunk but frankly I was not in the mood to break his lock just to find men's underwear.

In Nancy, we were housed in the university's dormitories. Since I'd never been in a dorm in the U.S., I didn't have an opinion about the accommodations. Frankly, in looking back, and after having stayed in many hotels over the years, I can say that the rooms in the dorm were larger than in some hotels where, when you opened the door, you fell out of the window.

Each room had the typical furniture of a student room and the bathrooms were in common areas in the hall. The only thing that we all had in the room was a sink and a bidet.

Needless to say, my American colleagues had no idea what a bidet was so it took some explaining. Therefore, along with French literature, they learned about French hygiene.

How did I know about bidets since I came from a village with an outhouse? Well, in Bucharest, where part of my family lived, every apartment had a bidet. Bucharest used to be referred to as Little Paris since many of the famous landmarks in Paris were duplicated in Bucharest. The fact is that all the aristocrats spoke French, much like the aristocratic characters in Tolstoy novels. Romania was quite Francophilic before the war and to this day, there is still a considerable vocabulary involving social relationships where French expressions are used instead of the Romanian terms - like *Merci* instead of *Mulțumesc* for Thank You and a few others with sexual connotations. The one that most amused me was when I learned the difference between the French and the English version. I guess it had something to do with British-French antagonism, probably dating back to the 100-year war. Who knows? But the word for condom in upper classes in Romania was "capote anglaise" which is French and means "English cap". On the other hand, when I lived in France, I learned that the Brits used the term "French cap" – no translation necessary. Go figure.

After I explained to my American colleagues the use of the bidet for hygiene "down under", and I don't mean Australia, they stopped using it as a toilet. At least the girls did; I can't vouch for the guys, since we were in separate dorms.

Fortunately, none of the French students were aware of this otherwise we would have had more than "Yankee Imperialist" graffiti on our room doors. The campus was overrun by leftists of all colors and persuasions after the student riots of the summer, and because the US was involved in Vietnam, we were easy targets.

But we really didn't care, we were really fascinated with the literature classes as we had never been exposed to the type of literary analysis we were learning at the University of Nancy. We realized that the essay, as used in American schools, had no structure, it was more or less stream of consciousness blabber, much like this memoir. French analysis was based on the classical approach and the difference between an *Explication de Texte* and a *Commentaire de Texte* was almost like learning to write based on a math formula. It was an extraordinary and gratifying experience.

Aside from our group of Americans, the majority was French students from small towns and villages around Nancy as well as several other foreign students but most interestingly, there were also two girls who were actually from Romania, but not refugees like me. I found that a bit odd, not to mention suspicious, since nobody could leave Romania for a vacation or any other reason during the Ceausescu regime. The only people who were allowed to travel out of the country at that time, and only under government supervision, were artists who performed abroad, athletes participating in international games, and the like. Certainly not "exchange students", though Romania did permit students from other countries to take courses in Romania especially in medical schools.

During Winter and Spring vacations, most if not all of the French students went home for the holidays but for us it was too expensive to go to the US, and most of our group simply stayed in Nancy, or took a trip to Paris or around the countryside.

Since I had just gotten my US citizenship that year and therefore had an American passport, I decided to take my Christmas vacation in Romania. I missed Romania so much, I really wanted to return for a visit. The fact is that I dreamt about Borșa almost every night since we arrived in the US. The dreams started several months after we settled in and began our new life. This was already after all the unpleasant incidents with the auto accident, school issues, President Kennedy's assassination, etc. It didn't have anything to do with not liking it here; I think it was simply the realization that we were settled in a new life, that I was no longer in my childhood place where I was so happy. My dreams were always about Borșa, never Vișeu, the town we lived in the last 3 years, as a teenager, before we left. Therefore it was really related to my happy childhood in Borșa. I had to go to Romania to get it out of my system, even though I was going to Bucharest, not my home town, but as they say, "You can take the girl out of Romania, but you can't take Romania out of the girl". Coincidentally, another student in our group from Queens College was also from Romania so Mariana and I decided to go together.

BORDER PROBLEMS – OR THE NEVER-ENDING TRAIN RIDES
One of the Romanian "exchange" girls mentioned above, upon hearing that I was going to Romania on vacation, asked me if I would do her a favor, since

she didn't have the money to go herself. The favor was to bring with me on my return, a small bag of books that her parents were going to bring to the train station when my train stopped in her town, Timisoara on the way back to France. I said yes, I'll bring you the bag.

Had I not had a US passport, I would not have even considered such a venture for fear that I would be detained in Romania since without the passport, I was technically stateless and on the radar of the Romanian Securitate (the local version of the KGB); and if I was in fact detained, nobody would be able to rescue me. As it turned out, this should have been the least of my worries.

So off we went. From the beginning, this decision did not seem too felicitous but I had no idea what a disaster was in store for me. And it had nothing to do with the Romanian police.

I saw the first bad omen soon after Mariana and I boarded the Wiener Walzer train to Bucharest that December 1968. The Wiener Walzer was much like the Orient Express, but it just didn't have the same allure as the Orient Express, probably because Agatha Christie hadn't written a book about a murder on its trains.

Anyway, unlike me, Mariana was not yet a US citizen and had only a US Re-Entry visa document which though it looked like a passport, was white and not blue like a US Passport. Its color gave it away immediately.

What followed could have been avoided had we done just a tiny itsy bitsy bit of research, like a phone call to 3 consulates to ask about requirements, namely, the consulates of the countries we were to pass through on the way to Romania which were Germany, Austria and Hungary. In our defense, it didn't occur to us that we needed a visa to go through by train since we had no intention of getting off in Germany or Hungary. But no, fearlessly, we set out on our journey as if we were going on a trip from New York to New Jersey.

Of course, as an American citizen I fared somewhat better, but suffered my own indignities.

The first casualty of our trip was Marianna. At the last station in France before the German border, officious and scary looking German patrols boarded the train to inspect travelers' documents. Remember, this was in 1968, before European Community relaxation of certain formalities. American citizens could travel through Western Europe freely, without visas. Permanent Green card residents like Marianna without an American passport were required to obtain a visa for every West or East European country they intended to visit. She did not have a visa for Germany. Without preamble, explanation, smile, or the slightest bit of compassion, she was literally hauled off the train with her luggage and left standing on the platform.

I was speechless. I was left alone on the train with the other passengers staring at me. As I waved good-bye to my friend, I got very uncomfortable. If I had not had relatives in Romania who were waiting for me, I would have gotten off the train as well and returned to Nancy with Marianna. But, I had some family obligation, so I continued.

But not for long. Little did I know that I would encounter a similar experience several hours later. This happened at the last train station in Austria before the Hungarian border. You know – at The Iron Curtain between West and East

Same scenario – Hungarian border police invading the train and I was expelled for not having a visa for Hungary. Why did I need a visa for Hungary even though I was just passing through on the train? Because unlike Germany and Austria which were West European countries, Hungary was a Communist country – they did not give a rat's tail about my American passport, but they did give me the option to obtain a visa at the border. So, off the train I went, with my luggage and was advised to take a taxi to the border where I would get the visa. Needless to say, I had to wave good bye to the Wiener Walzer as it waltzed out of the station on its way to Romania, without me.

To make a long story short, I did get a visa for Hungary, but by then, there were no more trains to Romania so I was advised to spend the night in a hotel and get on a train the next day. Since there were no hotels at the border, I took the next local train to Budapest and tried to get a hotel near the train station.

Now, I used to speak Hungarian pretty fluently until I started grade school in Romania. Though my Hungarian was rusty, and assuming that Hungarians didn't speak other languages, I decided to find my way around using Hungarian. I walked out of the station into the street and approached a policeman on a huge horse – a beast, I think it must have been one of those dressage horses with over built muscles, like the Lipizzaner stallions. He was enormous; I could have walked under that horse like walking under a ladder. The policeman was pretty intimating too, what with leather boots, whip and that uniform, he looked more like a Nazi than what I imagined Hungarians to look like – small delicate musicians or jovial pastry makers. This guy was not any of these. So I gathered up my courage and asked, *Nadyon sivenes, hogy van a hotel?* I thought I said, *"Please, can you tell me where there is a hotel?"* Much to my astonishment, and subsequent red face, he replied: *The hotel is very well, and how are you?* I guess I confused **where is** with **how is**. He then proceeded to give me directions to the nearest hotel which was about 500 feet away.

I checked in speaking Hungarian with no linguistic mishaps. When I got to my room I was shocked; the room was gigantic – I would estimate that it was about 900 square feet. I had never seen a room this size except when I lived in Vienna. What made it appear even bigger were the sparse furnishings – a double bed, a night stand, a table, an armoire and a sink. No bathroom.

The size of the room so dwarfed the sparse furniture, that the entire setting suddenly seemed comical. But I was not amused, I was mad. I was mad for having missed my train, for having lost all this time, for having to spend the night in a cathedral. I was hopping mad. Since the room had no bathroom, just a sink, I decided to pee in the sink instead of using the toilet in the hall.

So there. That was my revenge. I was also too terrified to sleep – that room was just too big. I thought that I might be invaded by an army. Ultimately I did fall asleep because I was simply exhausted from what I had to go through since leaving France that morning.

The next day I had a delicious breakfast and paid my bill - $2.00! Yes, 2 bucks for sleeping in that cavern. The breakfast was about fifty cents. By now I felt guilty about peeing in the sink, which was not an easy feat in the first place because I had to climb on a chair first to reach the sink. Oh well. I went to the train station and finally made it to Bucharest.

Snow wreckage

The visit with my family in Bucharest was very pleasant but the fear of talking about anything other than inanities because you never knew who listened through the walls and reported to the authorities that you had a capitalist from the evil empire of America in your apartment, was a bit tiring and frankly I couldn't wait to leave.

Besides, this was not even my town. I come from the Carpathian Mountains in the far North of the country, so being in Bucharest in the far South didn't bring back any memories at all, except for an earthquake when I was in a hospital in Bucharest because of some childhood disease. I remember the staff getting all the children out of bed and making us stay in the doorway of the room, as the tremors of the quake sent the hospital beds through the wall and landing on the grass outside. That was good advice, during an earthquake, stand in a doorway – it's the only structure that may not collapse.

On the way back to France, my cousin Harry took me to the train station and since it was January with lots of snow storms, the train was delayed. My cousin was worried that I'd be hungry on the train, so he bought me a large salami and stole a knife from the restaurant so that I'd have something with which to cut the salami. The salami was over a foot long but the knife looked more like a butter knife than something that you could cut meat with. Oh well, I didn't much care at that point, I just wanted to get out of there.

Because the train was 3 hours late, we arrived in Timișoara at 3:00 AM. This is where I was supposed to pick up that bag of books for the Romanian girl in Nancy. I did not think that her parents would still be there since the train was so late but there they were! And the bag with the few books? Right! It was gigantic Black leather suitcases that weighed a ton. By then, I was too tired to argue and embarrassed to refuse to take it because it was not what I was told, so I let the father come aboard the train and to my cabin and put the suitcase on the top luggage shelf. And they thanked me profusely. Oh well, I figured, who cares? The girl will come to help me with the luggage when I get to Nancy, in about 8 hours. Eight hours? Ha!

Here we go. The train got stuck several times because of the heavy snow fall before we even reached Hungary. Once we passed the border and were somewhere in the mountains, the train stopped for about an hour in the middle of nowhere. We were finally told that the train broke down and only the locomotive and 2 cars could continue. The rest of the cars had to be detached and abandoned.

Because I was in one of the last cars, I now had to get off the train, with 2 suitcases, and trek through about 3 ft of snow (the snow came up to my thighs) to one of the cars in the front. I was very lucky that another passenger, a man, helped with the second suitcase otherwise I would have had to make two trips in the snow to bring each of the suitcases to the front cars.

We finally made it to the front cars and settled in. By now there were fewer passengers and nobody bothered to store the luggage overhead. We simply left everything in the corridor.

The train finally made it to Vienna where it completely fell apart and was taken out of service. So now several of us who still had to continue to Germany and France were stuck in Vienna and tried to figure out how to get out of there. I must say that all travel in Europe was seriously disrupted during that awful snow storm so there were many people stranded.

After walking around the Vienna train station trying to find a train to Paris, I was approached by a man who told me that he was the conductor on the train to Strasbourg and that from there I could take another train to Nancy. He also offered me a sleeping car so I could rest since he knew about the ordeal I and several others had gone through in Hungary. I was very happy to hear this because I finally saw a light at the end of this disastrous tunnel. Not to mention that everywhere I went, I also had to lug two suitcases – it was about 20 years before rolling luggage was invented.

The only thing that made me uncomfortable about this man was that he spoke 3 languages at the same time: French, English and German. Since my German was not up to par anymore, I kept asking him if he preferred to speak English or French and he kept answering "yes". I asked "which – French or English" and he kept replying "yes".

I finally gave up and boarded the train and he did indeed place me in a sleeping car and said that he had to lock the door from the outside so the other conductors couldn't get in, especially since I did not have a sleeping car ticket. I said OK, because I was just too exhausted and I figured, what the heck can happen to me in a train? I mean I can always open the window and scream for help. In German. Hilfe!

Now sleeping cars are quite elegant and with many amenities such as sinks, toilets, towels, etc. But I still felt kind of uncomfortable – I don't know why. Maybe because I couldn't believe that this stroke of luck after such a disastrous trip could come without strings, or maybe it was a prelude to some other calamity. I may sound like a pessimist or even a bit paranoid but that's how I felt.

Therefore, I did not undress, or even take off my shoes but lay down on the bed fully clothed trying to take a snooze. But before that, I took the knife my cousin gave me out of my handbag and put it under the pillow while holding it in my hand.

Maybe about an hour later, I heard a knock on the door. I didn't answer since I assumed it was a conductor who was not supposed to know that I was in that cabin. But then I heard a key unlocking the door and sure enough it was my deranged multi-lingual controller who walked in. I pretended to sleep but watched him go toward the sink and look around, then come over to the bed and bend down near my face so close that I could smell his breath. My eyes were still closed but my hand was firmly gripping the knife under the pillow prepared to stab him in the stomach if he touched me in any way I considered dangerous. How I thought that I could defend myself with a butter knife is beside the point. Fortunately, he did nothing. Guess he just wanted to see if I was alive or something and since I was breathing normally, he felt I was safe and he left. Whew! That's all I needed, to be arrested in Germany for trying to kill a train conductor.

Unfortunately, this train didn't make it to its destination either. We had to get off in Stuttgart, Germany and after 2 hours of waiting on a frigid platform, we finally boarded a train that went to Strasbourg and Paris. By then, there were only 3 passengers left from the original train that departed Bucharest some 30 hours earlier.

The other two passengers were a Romanian lady and her young daughter. We started talking and she told me she was going to Paris where her husband was going to pick her up but because of this delay she didn't think he would still be there, and that she would have to take a taxi to his apartment. Her problem was that she had no money left - and the little she had was in Romanian lei as you could not get foreign currency in Romania.

I felt bad for her so I gave her $20 which was ample for a cab ride anywhere in Paris. She thanked me profusely and vowed to pay me back as soon as she got to Paris because her husband was Eugene Ionescu, a very famous Romanian playwright who lived in Paris. That's the only thing that stuck in my mind – Eugene Ionescu. He was part of that Theatre of the Absurd group like Samuel Beckett, Jean Genet, Harold Pinter and others. So to me, this was like a chance meeting with a relative of Mark Twain, or Ernest Hemingway. Needless to say, I never heard from her or anyone else named Ionescu so I think his estate owes me $20 -- forget the interest. I guess I was "absurd" to expect the payment. Sorry, couldn't resist this one.

THE PIG IN THE SUITCASE

I finally arrived in Nancy a couple of hours later after saying goodbye to Madame Ionescu and her daughter who stayed on the train to Paris.

Everybody at my dorm was scared that something had happened to me since I was supposed to have been back 3 days earlier. After I gave my friends some quick details of the train ride from hell, I immediately contacted the girl, Ana, whose books I schlepped all across Europe.

She appeared surprised that it was a suitcase and felt bad that I had to drag it around all this time, which I later realized was complete bullshit. She knew exactly what was going on. She invited me to her room for a drink and she proceeded to open the suitcase.

May I say that when I saw what was in it, I gagged on my drink, fell to the floor and almost choked to death. They beat me on the back until I coughed up the drink. What was in the suitcase was not books; it was an entire cooked pig in pieces, from head to tail. Having a pig at Christmas was a Romanian tradition, much like our turkey at Thanksgiving.

I nearly got killed smuggling a pig in a suitcase. Needless to say, after this story got around, I was the laughing stock of the entire school and taunted with various smuggling opportunities, none of them mentionable.

But I did learn one thing – never, ever, ever, ever agree to carry a package for someone without first looking inside.

I was (almost) a spy
The pig smuggling incident went in a different direction several weeks later and also put the Romanian girls in a different light.

Shortly after my exciting winter vacation, Ana, introduced me to 2 male friends of hers who were journalists for some Romanian newspaper. We had a couple of beers and talked about various things with many questions about my life in the US. I found this perfectly normal since, it appeared that everyone was fascinated by the US, especially if they had never been there.

Then, one of the men asked me if I'd be interested in writing articles about student life in France and when I returned to the US, continue in the same way, but focusing on student life in the US. He said that university students and people in general in Romania would be very interested in getting a glimpse of life in Western Europe and the US. They said I would be paid something like $50 per article. Needless to say, I was very impressed and flattered that they would offer me such a job, while I was still in college. One comment though should have raised a red flag, but I was young, impressionable and in the position of being offered a job before I even graduated so it kind of blinded me to the possibility of a more nefarious purpose he had in mind. The comment was that they were very impressed with my perseverance in dragging that damn pig through the mountains of Europe, therefore I was someone who was strong, reliable and loyal.

Notice, they didn't say anything about my journalistic skills, which were nil. Dissertations and other literary exercises, yes! After all that's why I was studying French literature, in France. But writing articles for a newspaper? Never did that, didn't even know what it entailed but I figured, how hard could it be?

In any event, I agreed and they told me that the first assignment would be given to me the following week. And they paid me in advance, in French Francs.

I was very excited and called my father in New York to tell him the exciting news. What followed was something I never knew my father was capable of; and that is a screaming voice that sounded as though he were going to have a heart attack.

What was it that so enraged him? The fact that he was certain these people were spies and were deliberately sent to France to recruit new victims because France was at that time in turmoil over the student revolution of 1968, which was a leftist movement and therefore fertile ground for recruiting for the KGB and other such agencies.

Most of my French friends at the university were engaged in some sort of left-wing activities which sounded almost comical. There were Maoists, Marxists, Trotskyists, Castroists – it was an endless list of "ists," some of which I had never even heard of. It was hysterical, if not pathetic mostly because they had no clue what philosophy or "ism" they were supporting.

For someone like me, who had lived under a communist regime, these people were like clowns, blindly quoting proclamations made by all of the above. Some even waved the little Red Mao Tze Tung book. It was quite amusing.

When I sometimes teased them by asking if they would like to move to one of the Eastern European countries like Romania to actually experience the "equality" they were so eagerly advocating, and where the portraits of Marx, Engels, Lenin and Stalin, their idols, were everywhere, in all public places, the reaction was not that enthusiastic.

Unfortunately, it wasn't only the students who were brainwashed. Many of the teachers were as well. For example, one of the teachers in my French literature class, a certain Monsieur Picard, insisted that all the writers we were studying should be analyzed in terms of how they portrayed "*l'idéologie de la classe dominante*", in other words, "the ideology of the dominant class". We were stumped – where the heck in Ivanhoe, or in Jerry Lewis movies does one find this ideology? In other words, at that time, every topic was cooked in the same sauce – *la sauce gauchiste*.

Needless to say, I came up with some excuse why I couldn't do the articles for my supposed Romanian employers. I began to understand how it works – first they get you to do some innocuous tasks like writing articles. Then they ask you for a different kind of "report". Little by little, they get a grip on you until it's too late to back out because they threaten to report you to the authorities. That's all I needed, to be an unwitting agent for a government that I despised simply because I was so flattered that they offered me a job while still in school. It turned out that the two women in my dorm were the advance recruiters - identifying potential candidates among the student body which they then handed over to the other agents. That was the end of my Mata Hari career.

I admit that over the years I have become suspicious and maybe even somewhat paranoid because I no longer believe in coincidences. Yes, there is good luck and bad luck and accidents happen. But when I think back on this experience I began to believe that everything that happened was not just bad luck but part of a plan to test me.

Maybe they were still after my father and tracked me to see if I might fall into their hands. But then reason took center stage and I realized that while the Communists and especially the KGB were good at covert operations, I doubt they had the technology to generate a snow storm that disrupted half of Europe. Or did they? Right, I was so important that it required a snow storm to test me. I really need to stop watching spy movies.

The rest of the year was quite uneventful except for sharing a table at a café in Paris with Jean Paul Sartre, at the Closerie des Lilas. As a French

Literature major, of course I knew about Sartre but the interesting detail of literature studies in France was that you could not study a living author in any course work. That was the rule at the Sorbonne so I suppose that all French universities followed the same rule. I have no idea what we talked about but I was mesmerized by the fact that I was sitting at a table with Jean Paul Sartre and of course, Simone de Beauvoir. It took me a while to get over it. Even now, whenever I'm in Paris and around the Boulevard Montparnasse, I think of them. My friends who were with me at the time were not literature majors so they were not quite as star struck as I was and they chatted a bit but they did tell him that I was American and studying French literature in Nancy. He asked me what I thought about French literature but I was so taken aback by this encounter, that I think I said something idiotic like "*C'est magnifique*". Mme de Beauvoir didn't say anything that I remember. He was very pleasant but a bit distant, just as I imagined he would be. I was glad he didn't ask me something political like the situation with the Vietnam war because I would have had to say that I didn't know anything about politics.

That is not what I used to say to all the French *gauchistes* on the college campus who tormented us about the war. I always responded with: "Listen, you "frogs" fucked up there and you dragged us in because you couldn't do the job; this is just the way we saved your ass from the Germans. So go ask your president why we are there." In French it was - oh never mind, I don't need to give French lessons in smut.

My end of year grade was the equivalent of a C+. I passed, but not with flying colors. And how could I? I spent most of the year drinking and carousing.

In fact, there was one class I never even attended – Latin. Why? Because it was the only class at 8AM and that's when the croissant truck came to deliver the croissants to the vending machine at the cafeteria. After a few days at the beginning of the term when I did attend the Latin class and came out at 9AM and saw the croissants gone, I decided that there was no point in being in France and missing the morning croissants. So it was Vale Adieu to the

Latin class and instead started stalking the truck. I used to stuff myself with at least 3 croissants every morning.

Then one day, we decided to follow the truck to see where he got the croissants, because the driver wouldn't tell us. So 4 of us, a NY colleague and two French guys got into their car and followed the truck as it drove out of the city to some small village outside Nancy. Once we saw the bakery, we decided to go there the next morning at 5AM because the bakery told us that the truck picked up the croissants at 6AM. This went on for a few days and then we got tired of getting up at 4AM just to eat croissants hot from the oven.

Did I pass Latin? Of course I did, and it was simply serendipity. One day, as I was sitting at the Excel Café near the train station reading a Romanian book while waiting for some friends, a man at the next table started to talk to me asking me about the book, which was a play by Ionescu, *La Cantatrice Chauve* (The Bald Soprano) which was kind of boring as I wasn't very enthused by the Theatre of the Absurd. Though I did name my cat Estragon, after a character in Becket's *Waiting for Godot*.

It turned out that this man was teaching Latin at the University. In fact, he was my teacher!!!!!! But since I was pursuing croissants at 8AM instead of "Sic transit gloria", I did not recognize him. So I sheepishly confessed my situation and conversed with him in Latin a bit so that he knew my background and promised to pass me if I came in the following week to take the final exam. I did, and passed, just barely. Whew!

KENT STATE UNIVERSITY CRISIS

After I came back from the study abroad year in France, I enrolled in graduate courses at Queens College for a Master's degree and was awarded a Lectureship, teaching French to first year college students which helped defray the tuition costs.

My classes in graduate school were quite interesting. They were certainly more serious than in undergraduate and one guest professor made me decide to change my major from French Literature to Linguistics. This was Noam Chomsky, the well-known MIT professor. His lectures were truly fascinating and I decided to apply to MIT where I was accepted but ended up not going because my parents couldn't afford the tuition and the housing. Oh well, I decided to get married instead.

One amusing experiment was the results of an essay we had to write for one of the courses. The professor knew that I spent the previous year in France so he graded my paper based on that knowledge. His comments on my paper were: *"This is the most brilliantly structured expose about …NOTHING! The year in France served you well.* **(A-)** *(If you had picked a real topic, it would have been A+)*

Ok, so I like to amuse myself, and others.

Now, as I mentioned, to pay for my tuition, I worked as a lecturer in freshman French classes. This was another one of those experiences that could only happen to me – I somehow seem to attract lunatics. I need to discuss this with my psychiatrist. So there I was on the first day of class with some 25 students. As was common in those days, I introduced myself as their French teacher for the semester, and wrote my name on the black board. Then I handed out index cards to everybody so they could write their names, their major and probably some other relevant information that I have forgotten by now.

The cards were then collected and as I read out each name, the student stood up so that I could connect the face with the name on the card; and I usually asked whether they had any specific questions or comments re the course. So far, so good.

Now, I got to a student named Judy Klein. She stood up and I noticed that she was dressed in a manly pants suit with a shirt and tie and a fedora hat. She immediately proclaimed that her name would shortly be changed to Marty and that I should call her Marty. I duly noted that on her index card and was about to go for the next card when she asked me my Zodiac sign. I asked her why she wanted to know that. She said it was to see if we would be able to get along. I said for her not to worry, that if she did her homework, we would get along famously.

That semester contained another eye opener for me about the education system in the US. These students, who were all obviously high school graduates did not know the first thing about English grammar. Since Romance languages are heavily based on verb conjugation and other strict grammatical rules, how could I teach French to people who didn't know what a pronoun was, or a possessive, or a past participle, etc.? It took me 2 months to teach them English grammar so that they could understand those grammatical terms in French. Well, no surprise – the same pathetic education I had myself already experienced.

But that was nothing compared to what came next. It started as a national tragedy and ended in a Kafkaesque comedy. It was 1970. The country was going through endless anti-Vietnam war protests on campuses all across the country. Then came the Kent State University demonstration that ended in a tragedy in which 4 students were shot by the Ohio National Guard.

Students across the country - even those at quiet Queens College – became enraged. Classes were cancelled while students demonstrated. It was total mayhem. Many of my students wanted to cut my classes; to avoid this, I suggested that we hold class outside on the grass. Seemed like a reasonable solution, as outdoor classes provided a "not business as usual" message and learning was not disrupted. Everybody was in agreement and that's what we did for several days.

Imagine my surprise when at the end of the semester, I got a notification that I was named as a defendant in a lawsuit brought by a student against several teachers at Queens College. The complaint was that we did not hold classes in a classroom during the campus protests.

I immediately contacted the dean who told me to relax, that this person sued all her teachers for the same infraction. And who was that student? None other than Judi (Marty) Klein. We ended up in court, five of us, and we were interrogated by the plaintiff's attorney regarding our decisions to cancel classes. Of course mine had not been cancelled, just moved outside. The judge dismissed the case and told Miss Klein to get a life and not waste the court's time with preposterous claims. Ms. Klein got a B+ in French.

Plane crash in Newfoundland

The following incident took place during Christmas vacation of 1970. I was flying to France for my 2 week vacation on Loftleidir Icelandic Airlines for a couple of reasons: Reason No.1, and the most important: it was the cheapest airline to Europe. Reason No. 2, after a stopover in Reykjavik, Iceland, it landed in Luxembourg which was much closer to the Moselle area where I was going to see my fiancé, then going through Paris. Yes, I was engaged to a Frenchman whom I met during my study abroad year.

Because this was just at the beginning of the winter recess, the plane was full of students, just like me. They drank like fish, and barely ½ hour after takeoff, everybody was drunk as a skunk. It was happy hour high in the sky.

Now, this plane was not a jet, it was a propeller plane. That meant that if your seat was near one of the wings, you could hear the engine rattling right through your body. That's where I was sitting, sober as a judge. Imagine that after about an hour, or maybe less, all of a sudden I heard the engine go silent. This was very strange and I looked around to the other passengers to see if anybody else noticed it. Obviously, they wouldn't have noticed it if the engine fell on their heads, they were so sloshed. After a few minutes, I summoned one of the flight attendants to ask if it was normal for an engine to go silent. She seemed a bit distracted but said that everything was OK.

Well, it wasn't OK because not 10 minutes later, the pilot advised over the loud speaker that we were making an emergency landing in Newfoundland because we lost an engine. We were asked to unbutton any tight clothes, and bend down with our face on our knees and hold on to our ankles. Five minutes later we crash landed in a remote area that was white as far as the eye could see. We were in the middle of nowhere. We also couldn't tell if the ground was ice or snow. But we were all OK, especially the drunk bunch, which I suspect was barely aware of what was happening.

The plane crew was very professional and caring, making sure that everybody was OK. Then they announced that we were to get off the plane through one of those evacuation slides and that some snow mobile type vehicle would take us to the nearest hotel where we would spend the night until the following day when a new plane would pick us up to continue our flight. The hotel was not far from where we landed and must have been totally unprepared for this unexpected avalanche of guests. They did their best to assign us two to a room, girls with girls, boys with boys.

The girl I was assigned with asked me if would be OK if she shared the room with one of the guys she met on the plane and have his assigned roommate share my room. How anybody could think of any bedroom antics after this adventure boggled my mind but who was I to judge. Of course I said, no problem, because at this point, I was so wiped out that I was prepared to share a room with Jack the Ripper.

As soon as I got to my room with that man, we shook hands and I plopped down on the bed and did not wake up until the next morning. Needless to say, I completely forgot there was a strange man in my room when I got up so we both got dressed (separately, in the bathroom), and we then started to get acquainted with each other by giving our names, discussing the whole adventure, and generally talking about what our plans were once we got to our destination.

Turns out this man was going skiing in France and Switzerland to get over a broken heart. Awwww. I agreed that it was a good idea to get away like this, that he'd have a lot of fun and who knows, he might meet many other nice girls. He said he was too heartbroken to even consider other girls because he would never find someone like his former love. Then he volunteered that her name was Ali McGraw. Hmmmm – if this had been any other time than having had to spend the night with a complete stranger in the next bed after a crash landing in the middle of nowhere in Newfoundland, I would have been all ears to hear more about this love affair with Ali McGraw gone awry. But my mind was elsewhere – like to get the fuck out of here. So I suggested we go and have breakfast because the plane would be arriving in about 2 hours.

The hotel must not have been prepared for such heavy traffic because all the food was either canned or from various concentrated sources. I had never had eggs from concentrate; I didn't even know such a thing existed. On the other hand, nobody could possibly complain; it was an unexpected bonus to get a free night at a hotel in the middle of nowhere in frozen Newfoundland. It's a place I always wanted to visit, in the dead of winter, of course.

After breakfast we were driven to an actual airport where our new plane was waiting and everything continued on schedule. I do remember that when we stopped in Reykjavik, we all bought Icelandic sweaters at the airport shop. Guess it was some sort compensatory act, or souvenir of our adventure. Unfortunately, after landing in Luxembourg, I never got around to hearing the end of the Ali McGraw failed love affair. We all scrambled away as fast as we could to our various final destinations.

My Wedding in France 1970

I got married in France in July of 1970 which in itself was somewhat theatrical as I was totally unfamiliar with the local laws.

I met my husband Riquet in college the previous year. I felt a bit guilty about getting involved with him during that school year while on the study abroad program because as I mentioned earlier, one of the reasons I went to France that year was that my American boyfriend was stationed in the army in Germany, so it seemed like a good idea to be closer to him.

Unfortunately, the heart doesn't always follow the mind but there was obviously another factor which did involve heart and mind and at least in my case, and that is how the mind influences the heart. I know this sounds rather convoluted not to mention obscure, but I think it comes down to chemistry.

The successful "chemical" combination for me, whether it involved men or women, was a sense of humor, wit and culture. That means that physical attributes did not play a big role in my attraction to men. Though Michael was my boyfriend in New York for a couple of years, I must say that I was not overly in love with him. He did not have any of the attributes above, though he was extremely attractive - a really very good looking guy. But I guess that wasn't enough.

When I met a number of the French guys during my year abroad, almost every one of them had the attributes that inspired me. So despite my dating several American boys during my college years in New York, none of them came close to sweeping me off my feet. Oh, and just if you're wondering, there was no sex ever with any of them. No sir, a little kissing here and there but that was it. I think it was just a different culture at the time. It was before the sexual revolution and all that Woodstock philosophy.

Anyway, however unpleasant, I broke up with Michael and became seriously involved with Riquet.

When I first met Riquet, I asked him what his real name was because I knew Riquet was a diminutive used for Henri in the south of France, not here in the north and the only thing this name brought to mind was King Henri IV who, however beloved as a king 500 years ago, was said to have smelled like a goat. So Riquet assured me he didn't smell like a goat and that though he lived in Nancy, he was born in the south of France where his father ran away during the war to join the Resistance. In fact, he was born one day before D-Day, in a small town near Bergerac.

Not only did he have a great sense of humor, smart, witty and with a French education, he knew more about the Bible Belt and the Corn Belt than I did, not to mention the names of the highest peaks in the Carpathian mountains. And he never set foot either in the US or Romania. Again - that pestiferous education element that seemed to plague me for years.

We got informally engaged in 1969 and got married a year later when I returned to France after my lectureship and master's degree classes at Queens College in New York.

The first surprise with respect to the wedding was a custom I was not familiar with, namely the "Publication des bans", or loosely translated, "Posting of the banns".

This is a public notice that has to appear several weeks before the wedding at the city hall of every town in France where a marriage is to take place thus announcing the impending marriage. The "banns" refer to any improper situation regarding the two individuals planning to get married. These can relate to being under the age of consent, or having been married before and not divorced, or any other condition that is would prevent a legal marriage in France. This is required so that anybody who objects to the marriage due to a legal issue can do it before the marriage ceremony takes place. The odd thing about this is that its roots are not in civil law but from religious practices from the middle ages. Considering that France practices true separation of church and state, unlike the US, one might think that this law is kind of archaic, well, really passé but it still serves a purpose.

When I say that there is true separation of church and state in France, I mean that, unlike in the United States, no priest, rabbi or any other religious cleric can perform a legal marriage. A marriage has to first be performed at the local city hall, and then you can have a religious ceremony.

Well, this part was of no consequence to me, they published the banns and fortunately nobody objected, we were both of age of consent and neither one of us was a bigamist.

The issue that was more complicated, not to mention absurd, was that I had no birth certificate since when we left Romania we were lucky we had a paper with our name on it. So to have a copy of our birth certificates would have been about as realistic as flying to Mars, or Pluto.

I had American citizenship and an American passport, what else did they need? They needed a birth certificate. Period. I explained why I could not provide a birth certificate and was told that since this is a required document, I could provide a document signed, sealed, notarized, certified and God only knows what other validations by witnesses who vouched that I was born on such and such a date.

Ok, so before leaving for France, I get these statements signed and notarized in New York according to the documents sent to me by the French government. The people who signed them were actually present at my birth -- an uncle and several other people including the doctor who delivered me.

Now I arrive in France with all these documents and it turns out they are not valid because the witnesses were not French citizens. Okayyyyy – now what? Well, very simple. The clerk told us to go out in the street, pick 2 strangers, offer them a drink and they'll sign any paper we want. And that's just what we did. In fact one guy was already so drunk, it took him several times to sign his name clearly, vouching under oath that I was born in Sighet, Romania on such and such a date! Hey, bureaucracy is the same everywhere.

I must also add that I really liked Riquet's family who were originally from Chateau-Salins, a small village in Moselle. One of the odd habits of some of the inhabitants there, at least at that time, was that they had these piles of dung right in the driveway next to the house, like where you would normally park your car. When I asked Riquet why that stuff was there, he said that they used it as fertilizer for the garden behind the house. Ok, so why keep the dung in the street instead of the garden behind the house? Well, because, they didn't want to ruin the look of the garden. Got it, that made a lot of sense, I guess that was French Moselle sense.

I especially liked Riquet's father, Eugene, who was a retired engineer for the coal mines in the area. He had a great sense of humor. They had a dog named *"Fous le camp"* after the name of a dog in a French comedy from the 1950s. *"Fous le camp"* means something like "Get lost" or "Scram". Therefore, whenever he called the dog to feed him, it would be: *"Fous le camp, viens ici"*, meaning "Get lost, come here". I think you have to be French to appreciate this.

The wedding took place at a charming inn outside of town as the owners were relatives of my husband's family.

Unfortunately, we found out 2 weeks later that the restaurant owner's wife ran off with the cook the day after our wedding – she didn't want to ruin our wedding plans. I thought that was very thoughtful of her. Was that a bad omen? Who knows.

France 1970-1972

I SPENT THE NEXT TWO years working at the Université de Nancy in a variety of capacities. I was also taking classes for the Maitrise degree (Master's Degree) in linguistics. The curriculum included a long list of languages from which we could choose at will – none were specifically required for the degree. After Latin and Greek I decided to take something called Fortran – I had never heard of this language, and I thought it was something like Esperanto or Aramaic. The shock of seeing those huge IBM mainframes on the first day of class, and the punch cards, was a bit disconcerting but I was too embarrassed to bow out. So that was my first experience with computers – I hoped to never see one again. Why the university would list computer programming "languages" as part of a Linguistics curriculum along with real languages, however ancient or archaic, was rather bizarre, but then who was I to judge? I was so impressed with the level of education in France that this was nothing more than a minor hiccup. Little did I know how well it would serve me some 20 years later.

To make some extra money I also taught English classes at various subdivisions of the university, translated abstracts at international symposia like Rock Mechanics (Rock Mechanics?) and a stint at a science lab at the Centre de Médecine Préventive (Center for Preventive Medicine). I also did a stint in a junior high class replacing the teacher who was on maternity leave. This went well and was a great learning experience about French culture which is: when it's mushroom season, do not expect the kids to come to class – they're all out with their parents collecting mushrooms. I suppose this was the mushroom version of "*vendange*", when it's grape picking season. I think the entire country disappears, somewhere in Beaujolais, Bordeaux, Bourgogne and other wineries.

The only unpleasant part of those two years was an incident at the École Commerciale where I was teaching a course in Marketing – in English. What did I know about marketing? Nothing! But I read a few books and shared them with the class – all in English of course. I realized that English was replacing French as the lingua franca. Everything had to be translated into English, so if you aspired to any career in business or science, you really needed to know English.

The unpleasant incident which made me lose about 15 pounds in two weeks from stress, fear and lack of sleep was that shortly after I started teaching the class, I was harassed by a stalker who kept leaving messages under my apartment door. The messages were all addressed to me and they were all creepy love letters.

I would sometimes find the notes in the morning before I left for work, sometimes in the afternoon when I was in a class and sometimes in the evening when I came back from dinner in a restaurant. The fact that this person knew where I lived and was actually outside my door in the middle of the night or any other time of the day, simply freaked me out.

Naturally, we went to the police but what could they do? Since we lived in a public housing building, le Haut du Lievre in Nancy, the police said that there were probably some unsavory characters living in my building. They also asked me if I was ever in contact with people who were just acquaintances, and not close friends. I couldn't think of anybody except people I knew vaguely from school or the course I was teaching.

So I was trying to think who this could be when one day, another note appeared under my door which finally gave the writer away – it was one of my students because of a reference he made about a jacket I wore in class that day. And this was a frightening note. No more love – now he wanted to strangle me like a rabbit and kill my cat Lucifer. I guess he could hear the cat meow behind the door but why he referred to the poor thing as Lucifer, I didn't understand. My cat's name was Moujik, but he obviously didn't know that.

But which student was it? Since the notes were hand written, I decided to look at the index card each student filled out at the beginning of the semester to see which one matched the handwriting. I could not find any match.

Then Riquet, decided to look at the cards by himself. It took him two minutes to find the match.

Why was he able to find it out and not I? Because he didn't know these students, and when he looked at the handwritings he could be objective about it. I obviously was not objective because as I looked at the name on a card I visualized that person and thus made judgments based on the personality of the individual. There was nothing about any of my students that was in any way out of the ordinary. Since the handwriting was indeed a perfect match, I was shocked when I realized who it was.

This young man was the quietest one in the whole class. He always sat in the back, and never participated in any discussion. Sometimes it looked as though he was dozing but I never really paid attention to it. Unlike high school where teachers need to engage students in question and answer exercises, in college it doesn't work that way, at least not in France. College students attend classes and participate at will. Of course, at that time, I had not seen enough crime shows on TV to realize that there was such a thing as a sociopath. That's what this young man was. When I went to the college administration and showed them the letters, the cards and related the entire history, they were extremely disturbed.

They called the police and the student was arrested. He was going to be interrogated the following day and they asked me to attend the meeting. They asked him many questions based on some of the content of the letters. His answers made it difficult for everybody to refrain from exploding in hysterical laughter. This young man was a certified wacko.

Some of the answers were:

- He fell in love with me because I spoke French with a Lebanese accent. Come again? Lebanese????
- My clothing drove him crazy - the black turtleneck sweater, black pants and red ski jacket. He maintained that I knew that the color combination of Red & Black excited him. (Maybe he was a Stendhal fan from *Le Rouge et Le Noir*?)
- He called my cat Lucifer because the cat was the devil that got between me and him (Huh?)
- He didn't really want to strangle me like a rabbit, but since I lived at Haut du Lievre (Hare Heights) he thought it was appropriate – rabbit, hare, same thing.

After the interrogation he was let go with the admonition that he was not to have any contact with me and he was suspended from my class. I was subsequently told that in reviewing his file, the school staff found documents to the effect that this young man spent 6 months in a mental hospital two years before entering the university.

Although the university administration was very supportive of me in this incident, they nevertheless told me at the end of the school year that they would no longer appoint women as teachers at this particular division because of this incident. Although this decision did not affect me because I already had another job, I thought how utterly French that decision was! It wasn't quite blaming the victim, just a very creative way to hide behind blatant sexual discrimination. I guess they had a few more loonies in the student body and just wanted to avoid any more criminal incidents.

French Police

Speaking of police, I had several encounters with the police in Nancy, all of them amusing for them but causing fear and embarrassment for me. The first one was the incident with the loony student.

The second one was mortifying for me. I had just learned how to drive a stick shift in a Renault 4 and I accompanied my husband in the car as he drove to his military base in Toul which was about 20 km from Nancy. After he got out of the car, and since the engine was still running, I had no problem driving back to Nancy.

I drove to a café where I was meeting some friends and parked the car at the curb. The café was at Place Stanislas, the main plaza in Nancy, a superb area surrounded by Black and golden spiked gates and elegant 18th century buildings including the Royal Palace and the Government Palace. Place Stanislas was named after a mix of Dukes of Lorraine, the last one being Stanisław Leszczyńsk who was related to Louis XV. Outdoor cafes abounded on all sides of the square so it was a very popular hangout. That evening, there was a parliamentary meeting at the Government Palace and the province's parliament deputy, Jean-Jacques Servan Schreiber, was in attendance.

After some chitchat and a *café au lait*, I was ready to leave the café because I was tired and just wanted to go home. Unfortunately, I couldn't figure out how to start the car. I didn't know how to use the clutch, so that each turn of the key produced something like an explosion and the car jumped forward and then back but I could never turn on the engine. My friends sitting at the tables outside were in stitches screaming *"Agiter avant de s'en servir"* (Shake before using) but nobody thought of coming to help me.

While I was shaking, rattling and rolling the car, many people crossed the square in my direction and I saw Mr. Schreiber and others glancing at my car. At that moment, two policemen came over and asked what my problem was. By then I was in tears and explained that I didn't know how to start the car because of the clutch and that I was an American not used to driving a stick shift.

Figure 9 - Riquet, in front with tie, and our friends in Nancy

While they both struggled to avoid laughing, one of the policemen told me to move to the passenger seat so that he could get into the car and showed me how to start it by keeping the left foot on the clutch, with the right foot on the gas pedal and turning the key to start the engine. He then turned off the engine, and asked me to start it, and I did. Whew! He then told me to please drive carefully and try to not kill anybody on the way home, especially the province's deputy and wished me a Bonne Soirée.

During this whole time, my friends were still laughing hysterically and by now the scene attracted a bunch of onlookers whom I heard explain to each other, *"C'est une américaine qui ne sait pas conduire avec un levier de vitesse"* (It's an American who doesn't know how to drive a stick shift).

Fortunately, I made it home without running into or over anyone and the next day I managed to start the car with no problem. Another great accomplishment – learning how to drive a stick shift! I was very proud of myself.

Another minor police interchange was one I initiated. I was about to park the car near the Excel restaurant at the train station when another car passed me by and because he was probably upset that I "stole" his parking place, rolled down his window and called me a *"sale boche"*. He then proceeded to park his car 5 cars ahead of me.

I saw a policeman and approached him to complain that the guy, there, that blond Aryan getting out of a Peugeot, called me a "sale boche". The policeman asked me which was my car and I showed him the Renault 4. He looked at the licence plate and said " *Ah, oui, malheureusment, il y a des imbeciles en Lorraine qui pensent que la Moselle est en Allemagne*" – "Ah yes, unfortunately there are imbeciles in Lorraine who think that the Moselle county is in Germany".

So what was this all about ? "Sale boche" is hard to explain because we don't have this particular pejorative term, though it may exist in England. It's something like "dirty kraut" - a nasty reference to a German. Now, why would this guy call me a "dirty kraut"? Because the license plate of Riquet's car was issued by the county of Moselle which borders Germany, and therefore it was like an "out-of-state" license plate and it was well known that many of the inhabitants of that region spoke a German dialect in addition to French. The policeman went over to the guy who was about to enter a bistro, stopped him and asked him to apologize to me because I was neither dirty nor German. He told the guy I was an American studying in France and I was driving a friend's car. The guy turned kind of purple and quickly apologized and offered to buy me a beer. I told him I didn't drink and drive but I'd take him up on it some other time. Never saw him again.

The next experience I had with the police was serious. Both Riquet and I were arrested for burglary. Frankly, if I ever found myself in the same situation again, I would commit the same crime with no thought of the consequences, like being arrested.

At the time, in 1972, we were planning to move to New York. But we also had the cat, Moujik, whom we of course wanted to take with us. Unfortunately, after much investigation it turned out that the cat would have to be in quarantine for 6 months in the US before they would allow us to bring her home. That just didn't sit well with us. One week, two weeks, OK – but 6 months?

Absolutely not. So we decided that we needed to find someone who would be willing to take the cat. We found a nice couple who lived not far from us who said they would be happy to adopt the cat.

About a week after the cat was gone, I missed her and wanted to see her. We went over to their apartment and knocked on the door and there was no answer, but I heard the cat meow. So then we walked down to the concierge and asked her if the couple upstairs was around or just out or whether they were away. Remember, nobody had phones at the time so there was no way to check in advance. The concierge told us that the couple was away on vacation for two weeks, in St. Tropez!

We asked her if she was taking care of the cat or whether someone else was coming over to feed the cat. She said nobody had been by since they left which was about 4 days earlier, which meant that these creeps knew they were going away a few days after they took the cat. There was no rush, they could have told us that they would take her when they got back from vacation. So it was our luck to find out before it was too late what kind of despicable people they were.

I was simply horrified. Riquet was also very upset but tried to hide it so as not to make me more upset. We went home and decided that we would come back at night and get the cat. And that's what we did.

It was around 1:00 AM and we snuck upstairs without the concierge hearing us, broke the lock on the door and went in. There was a large bowl of food and water but certainly not enough for 2 weeks – the food bowl was half empty and so was the water bowl. We grabbed the cat, wrapped her in a blanket and scooted out. I don't know how the concierge found out that we broke into that apartment, but she called the police and they asked us to come down to the station the following day. I must say it didn't bother me one bit, I was happy to explain what we did and why.

The explanation was very simple. We couldn't bear the fact that these people, after taking the cat, instead of trying to familiarize her with her new environment, befriend her, cuddle her and make her feel at home, took off to St Tropez instead leaving her all alone with just food and water which was gone after barely 2 days. There is no question that cats can survive a rather long time with little food, like when they run away and hide in a truck or something like that. But this planned cruelty committed by these 2 people was simply unconscionable.

So after the explanation, instead of being charged for burglary we were told that they understood perfectly why we did what we did and that there would be no charges, but that we had to pay for the broken lock on the creeps' door. We paid. After the creeps came back from vacation, they avoided us like the plague. But one time I ran into the woman at a supermarket and while she pretended not to see me, I passed by her and without looking at her I said in a loud stage whisper – MEOW! Yup, I can be a bit of a bitch – but only when it's well deserved.

After this incident that the entire town knew about, an older couple contacted us and said they would like to take the cat. He was an accountant and she was a teacher and they had two children. They promised to take the cat with them every time they went on vacation, which was usually in August of course, when the whole country shuts down as everybody is off on summer vacations to the South of France. Well, maybe some go to Deauville. So they took the cat and for years after that, they kept sending us pictures of Moujik in their apartment being cuddled by the children, Moujik in the back seat of their car, Moujik on a terrace in St Tropez – it was just fabulous! They loved the cat and used to write to us about all the mischief she used to get into.

One bit of mischief that I knew very well and warned them about was that she used to eat all our shirts and sweaters if left on the bed or on a chair. She specialized in underarms – every shirt and sweater in the house had large underarm holes. She also used to eat the tip of every sock my husband took off as well as the buttons on his shirts and his shoe laces. In fact, she used to eat anybody's shoe laces, such as guests who would sit at our dinner table and didn't pay attention to the cat under the table, until they got up and fell out of their shoes. Yes, the cat was a bit of a lunatic but she ended up having a wonderful life and died at the ripe old age of 19.

The last French police encounter I remember was in Paris also in 1972. Riquet and I were driving to Paris for a few days in our crappy Renault 4. By the time we got to the outskirts of the city, we began to notice that something was wrong with the car but couldn't quite figure out what it was. We stopped on the side of the main road and Riquet opened the hood to look in but of course, he was not a mechanic, so he couldn't tell anything. It was just making a funny noise. So we continued but by the time we got to the bridge that connects to the Isle Saint Louis, the car was beginning to make a louder choppy noise so Riquet decided that we should just stop and see if we could find a garage.

As we made the right turn off the bridge, the Pont de la Tournelle, onto Isle St Louis, the car started smoking fumes and we just parked in the first space available, on the river side. As we stopped the car, there was a little explosion and the car just went dead, but still fuming at which point we just jumped out of the car fearing a fire, or worse, an explosion.

In the blink of an eye, within about 20 seconds, we were surrounded by 3 men whom I saw getting out of the car that was parked behind us. One man remained in the car at the wheel, just watching. They asked us what the problem was and we both explained, scared out of our wits. They looked at the car and said there was no cause for alarm, it would not burst into flames, it was just some engine trouble. Then they called for help on some kind of walkie-talkie and stayed with us until the truck came.

We thanked them profusely for being of such quick help and wondered how lucky we were to find such helpful people, sitting in a car, as if just waiting for us. After they understood that we were not exactly dangerous, just some students from out of town in a crappy car, and one American, they told us that they were always parked in this spot because it was in front of the building where … Georges Pompidou lived! The President of France! Well, it was actually his wife's apartment. They were the French secret service, and exploding cars in front of the President's home was kind of unsettling, to say the least. We then decided that as soon as we got back to Nancy, we were getting a new car, or else. The "or else" came from me.

Romania 1972

As I mentioned, by 1972 we had decided to move to New York, mainly because I was bored with the lifestyle, I missed my family and friends but most of all, I did not see any career opportunities in France at that time other than being a teacher. Not that I didn't like teaching, but after the incident with the psycho student it just seemed that teaching was so limiting. After all, I had summer jobs in New York that were more interesting. Also, at least at that time in France, it was nearly impossible to get into any other kind of business without taking endless courses like the guys who were specialists in hammering nails, that required certificate to hammer nails, the CAP (*Certificat d'Application Professionelle*), was just not my style. Plus, what was it they always said about the US? The US was the land of opportunity! We decided to move to New York.

Before we left Europe for good, I wanted to go to Romania one more time, this time with Riquet and by car which makes for a much more enjoyable trip. Yes we did get a new car, a Simca 1000.

When I told my parents, they said that my sister wanted to come too, as well as my cousin, who was born in New York, and therefore had no idea where her family came from also wanted to come. So Shari and Karen came to France, and we all embarked on this road trip across eastern France, Switzerland, Austria, Hungary and into Romania.

This time we went straight up the mountains to our home town in Borşa, passing through Vişeul de Sus where we lived the last 2 years before we left Romania. It was only 10 years since we had left the country and nothing much had changed other than once in a while we did see a car on the road, though mostly still herds of cows, sheep, goats and horse drawn carriages. As I said, not much had changed. The whole trip was planned like an adventurous excursion, meaning that we had no idea exactly what the itinerary would be, where we would stay overnight, the condition of the roads, nothing.

This was just like the time we went on vacation to Ouagadougou, in Upper Volta, now Burkina Faso, in Africa. How did we end up there? As teachers we of course had 3 months' vacation and after having toured France and other European countries, one summer we decided to pick a place by rotating a globe with our eyes closed, and wherever our fingers stopped on the globe, that's where we would go. Smart, right? That's how we ended up in Ouagadougou. It was interesting, but not funny!

Anyway, back to our journey to Romania, this time, my biggest fear was finding gas stations since driving was not yet common in Eastern Europe, except for trucks but somehow we managed and it helped that our new car, the Simca, was very fuel economical. The fact that some of the roads weren't paved and that we had to push the car over rocks and boulders, was a different story. The other issue was that the few gas stations we did find did not have the amenities they have today. So when nature called while we were on the road, we just stopped the car on the side of the road and went into a bush. With me it happened as we were driving along a river so when we stopped and I went into a bush to do my thing, a frog jumped on my derriere, which was OK, I was used to frogs. At least it wasn't a bear.

After we visited friends in both towns and stayed in some "hotel" full of bedbugs, we turned south to go to Bucharest and the beach, on the Black Sea. I had been there several times with my parents back in the early 50s when my father was still a big cheese in town, and before things got really nasty.

The trip south was amusing since we did not have a lot of money and instead of staying at hotels on the road, which by now we tried to avoid for fear of bedbugs, we stayed with families in private houses. The one I remember well was in Timișoara where we stopped at a gas station and a man approached us and asked if we were going to a hotel. Since I was the only one who could speak Romanian, I said that we didn't know yet where we were going, which was the truth. The entire trip was a haphazard adventure. He told us that we could stay at his house for some ridiculously low figure which also included breakfast. So we followed him.

Apparently, it was a custom in larger towns that local people would hang out at gas stations and lure tourists traveling on the cheap which allowed them to make some money. Everything was fine until my sister and my cousin saw the man chopping wood with an ax in the courtyard. Both started having visions of Dracula and were convinced that he was planning to kill us in the middle of the night so they just wouldn't go to bed. Why he would want to kill us was never explained by the 2 teenagers who saw too many stupid movies. Needless to say, we were all alive and well in the morning and were served a nice European breakfast with homemade blackberry jam.

The trip to the Black Sea was uneventful other than when we went to Eforie to try out the mud baths. We ran into a little problem with a group of angry people which was typical under Communist rule. It was really very sad to see so many of these people in large cities picking fights with each other over real or imagined offenses. The point is people just seemed angry and this was certainly understandable considering the conditions under which they were living and the daily deprivations they had to endure.

In our case, it was a mob of naked women who tried to attack us, or rather me. Since men and women were in separate areas while smearing their bodies with mud, my husband Riquet did not see this incident.

The issue was that I took a picture of my naked sister and cousin covered in mud and leaning against a wall. Since the women heard us speaking English, they immediately assumed, correctly, that I was American. I don't know why they didn't think that my sister and cousin were American too, since we all spoke English. It's just one of those things that when you're on a crusade, it doesn't matter what the reality is, you just want to battle. In other words, " We've made up our minds; don't confuse us with the facts".

So these naked mud covered ladies started surrounding me and screaming accusations that I was an American taking pictures of poor Romanian girls for an American porno magazine. Actually, that wasn't all that far-fetched as I'm sure that given the oppressive conditions and general poverty, some ladies probably took advantage of tourist "offerings".

After all, we came into the country prepared with several pairs of jeans, pantyhose, soap, toothpaste, cologne, Kent cigarettes and other ordinary products that you could find anywhere in Western Europe but not in Romania. These we sold to anybody who asked for them. In fact, we got through Customs by giving the agents several cartons of Kent cigarettes to entice them into not checking the contents of our suitcases. What the obsession with Kent cigarettes was, I don't know. I think that was the only brand one could buy in the one store in Bucharest that sold products for foreign currency. And no Romanian was allowed in there lest they end up you know where. The punishment for a Romanian possessing dollars was immediate arrest and God only knows what then happened to them. This was after all the Ceausescu regime.

Unfortunately for these ladies, who yelled their accusations in Romanian, they didn't know that I had a nastier mouth than they did in Romanian. After I translated the accusations to the girls they cracked up and asked what I was going to tell the crowd. I said: Watch me.

I turned around to face the angry crowd of naked women – sorry I just couldn't get over the comedy of belligerent naked women - and said very calmly in Romanian:

"Dear ladies, if you don't go back to whatever you were doing before you started surrounding me while I was taking a picture of my American sister and cousin, I will tell the police outside the gate here, that you have all asked me if we would sell you some dollars because you noticed that we're American".

Except for the fact that these ladies had no tails between the legs, their retreat was rather spectacular, almost as if it had been staged, complete with dirty looks. It almost looked like a medieval war scene where an army retreats with their swords and other war time paraphernalia, except these were naked women. I still can't get over the vision. Oh, and by the way, I still have that photo of the 2 naked teenagers covered in mud. I'm keeping it just in case either one of them wants to use it as a TBT on Facebook. That should generate some LIKEs, SHAREs or get them banned by Facebook.

As if this was not enough to make us leave the area, the next day we all got sick and decided to drive back to Bucharest for a day or two and then back to France. Unfortunately, on the road back to Bucharest, the illness got worse and we had to stop the car every few kilometers to relieve ourselves. We thus left souvenirs all over the corn fields and other pastoral spots until we got to Bucharest and went straight to a hospital. It tuned out that we all had dysentery from something we ate in Constanza. Riquet was hospitalized immediately but they let us out with some medicine because we were not as severely ill as he was. The next day when I came to visit him, they wouldn't let me in because he was in a quarantined section with others suffering from the same thing.

Apparently, overnight, about 20 more people were hospitalized with the same condition. The only way I could talk to him was through the window from outside. He was hopping mad screaming that they put in a bed with another man, a gypsy! I couldn't believe it, two people in one hospital bed? Oh well, they obviously ran out of beds.

I tried to speak to the doctor in charge especially since Riquet didn't speak Romanian but the doctor wouldn't see me. So I called one of my friends, Speranța, who I knew was very "connected" with various government officials. She called the Minister of Health; yes, the actual Minister of Health for the whole country and he told her he would pick us up at 10PM and take us to the hospital. He did indeed do that, and rather than having a chauffeur, he was driving the car himself. I must admit that during the ride I was praying that I would live through this and not die before we got to the hospital. It's not that I was sick, but the man drove like a maniac, I never saw anybody take a street turn at 60 miles per hour so that the car turned on its side riding on only two wheels. I was totally freaked out.

Fortunately we made it to the hospital without killing anybody or ourselves. My friend and I waited outside until the Minister came out. He said that my husband would sleep in the doctor's office that night, on some kind of makeshift bed and he would be released the next day if we promised to get out of the country immediately. When I asked him exactly what was wrong with my husband, he said, "How the hell should I know? I didn't look up his ass". OK.

The next day he was released from the hospital and we took off and made it to Vienna in one day without eating anything, because at that point we were terrified of food in Communist countries, as if the disease had a political aspect to it. It was just bad luck. The first real meal we had was in Vaduz, Lichtenstein - huge steak with French Fries. It felt so good to be safe again. And we all lost 15 pounds in the space of 4 days.

Casablanca

During the late 70s – early 80s I spent a lot of time in Morocco as Riquet was in the travel business and his company had an agreement with Royal Air Maroc about promoting tourism to Morocco from the US.

It was always fun and I made a lot of friends there and learned a lot about local customs. In fact, I used to host dinners for the airline staff at our apartment making couscous from scratch which left my kitchen full of couscous crumbs for days since it was such a messy process. The lamb and figs or prunes were much easier to deal with. The airline people always brought the dessert, straight from Casablanca – the briouats, a delicious pastry. Since I used to just hang around the hotel in Casablanca while Riquet was in business meetings, I saw a lot of people coming and going. One day I saw the staff lay out a long red carpet in front of the entrance which was reserved for VIP guests. I asked one of the employees if he knew what VIP was coming today and he said it was a prince from Saudia Arabia.

I should have known it was someone with lots of moolah since the elevators were stuffed with cases of Chivas Regal, champagne and other treats fit for a wedding and the entire top floor was reserved for him. I didn't see the prince come in but when I went down again from my room, there was a young man sitting on one of the lobby sofas with a big leather portfolio. I thought he might have been an architect but when I started talking to him he said he was part of the prince's entourage. I asked him about the portfolio and he showed it to me – it was a portfolio of the prince's wardrobe – swatches of every suit fabric, shirt, tie, pocket square, shoes, everything. He said that this was what the prince used to decide what he would wear at any time of the day.

I didn't see the prince or his entourage during the few days they stayed at the hotel but on the day he checked out, his assistant came to the reception desk with a briefcase filled with packs of hundred dollar bills and paid in cash. As he was waiting for the entourage to come down, he showed me the prince's passport – I think he realized that I was just a bored housewife so I was no danger. I loved the passport – I won't divulge his name but under "Occupation" it was marked: "Cousin du Roi" – The King's Cousin! Now that's a nice occupation.

Again, no names since they're all still around and I knew them because I was in the fashion industry and worked with some of them, but the day after the prince arrived, a group of 6 well known models from New York came to the hotel in Casablanca and they all stayed on the top, royal floor. It's good to be a prince!

I believe the royal entourage went to Marrakesh for a few days and then to New York because who was sitting in front of me several days later on the Royal Air Maroc flight but His Highness. This was the first time I actually saw him in person. He had a terrible headache and the airline staff didn't have any aspirin, but I did. I gave him my bottle, and after he took the aspirins, he got up from his seat to give me back the bottle, and thanked me for my generosity, in French, and gave me …. an emerald ring as a thank you. I was shocked but I behaved myself. I knew that you cannot refuse a gift, that it's an unforgivable insult. I did say it was not necessary, that I was happy to help but he insisted, staring straight into my eyes. I accepted the ring and thanked him profusely. Le Cousin du Roi of Saudia Arabia was indeed a gentleman, definitely a prince.

East Hampton

I will be making several references to East Hampton so I might as well explain how I ended up there in the first place. I have been there since the mid-70s largely because of Riquet's obsession with fishing. He was an avid fisherman his whole life in France but living in Manhattan, it's not that simple to go fishing. After trying out Sheepshead Bay in Brooklyn and some other locations around Queens, he just didn't like it, especially when he saw a man of war for the first time – he freaked out. He thought it was some prehistoric creature. So did I, we did not have men of war in Romanian rivers.

A friend of his mentioned that the best place to fish is in a place called Montauk which is at the eastern end of Long Island. Of course I never heard of "the Hamptons" but I had been there once before, the summer before I went to France looking for a summer job. I needed a summer job before I left so that I would have some money but I was bored with typical garment area companies and was looking for something more fun, like a job at the beach. I applied for a job as a maid a Gurney's Inn but didn't get the job. They hired a lot of the kids who were there like me, but not me. I guess they thought that maybe I don't know how to hold a broom. Who knows?

Anyway, we went to Montauk and stayed with some French friends who rented a cabin and Riquet simply fell in love with the area. I even went on one of the fishing boats with him, one of the Viking Fleet of commercial fishing boats that are very popular for ocean fishing. Unfortunately, even though I didn't get seasick, I had an unpleasant experience that cured me of fishing altogether.

First of all, fishing is just not part of my DNA – I don't know, Jews just don't seem to fish. At least not where I came from despite the beautiful pristine rivers we had all around us. The whole concept was a bit out of my universe. But the final straw was when on that Viking ship, which carried a bunch of fishermen, one of them caught a huge bass and as he hauled in on to the deck, it hit me on the head and knocked me out cold. That was the final straw. As much as I wanted to be supportive of Riquet's fishing obsession, I decided it just wasn't for me. So he went fishing by himself late at night off Gann Road on one of the bays and kept bringing back those small blue fish that just grossed me out. I hate cleaning fish. Then one night, as he was still not back by 3AM and I didn't have a car to go look for him, and no, we didn't have cell phones in the 70s, I had to call the police to look for him. I was right to worry – he fell off the dock into the water because he caught something very heavy. In trying to haul it in, he lost his balance and fell in the water. What was this huge fish that knocked him off the dock? A truck tire! The policemen brought him home drenched and stinking and probably laughed their heads off when they left. I can just imagine what they were thinking: "dumb frog falls in the water while fishing!"

The following year we rented a house with the same couple in Amagansett on Hedges Lane. It was a perfect location, a short walk to Indian Wells Beach and an even shorter walk to Main Street and The Stephen Talkhouse, the local hot spot night club. What else do you do after a day of fishing? Drink beer and enjoy live music.

After a couple of years of sharing a rented house in Amagansett, both we and our house mates decided to buy houses instead of renting since it seemed that all four of us loved this area and it just didn't pay to keep renting. So we all set out to look for a house, separately, of course. Riquet and I found a very nice ranch style house in the Springs area of East Hampton.

It turned out we were neighbors of Willem de Kooning but we had no idea until one rainy November when my car, skidding on a pile of wet leaves, crashed into his gate. He had a strange sense of humor because as I went in to apologize and offer to pay for any damages, he said to me "There are easier ways to meet me than to crash my gate". I had no idea what he was talking about, he had a slight foreign accent that I couldn't make out but he never told me who he was. He just said there was no damage so I didn't have to do anything. It was weeks later I found out who he was. Too bad I never got to see his studio.

The other surprise was that our friends found a house … right next door to us! We were next door neighbors which made for much fun and entertainment. Our friends also inherited some chickens from the previous owners so we had fresh eggs every weekend. We all had a great time.

But before any of these events, the actual move to our new house in East Hampton was marred by the kind of accident that fortunately didn't hurt anybody physically, only our dignity. We moved in with a bang - literally.

Riquet decided that we should just rent a truck and put some furniture in and other household items and do it ourselves. I don't remember if it was an issue of saving money or that Riquet thought he was one of those guys that can do everything himself. I believe it was the latter since the acquisition of the house was not much of a financial burden. The house cost $40,000 and it came with an assumable mortgage of $20,000 at 5% which meant that our monthly mortgage payments were about $150. Totally doable since we both had jobs and no other expenses. My parents helped with the down payment. Don't ask what an assumable mortgage is: it's an extinct financial animal today.

So here we are, driving this rented truck to East Hampton, and as we get to the underpass bridge on North Main Street, the inevitable happens. The top of the truck hits the bridge and the truck gets stuck. Needless to say, we are now surrounded by police cars and various other vehicles. I remember that somebody started to deflate the tires so the truck was lowered below the level of the bridge and then a tow truck helped us get to our destination. The top of the truck was completely shaven off.

We got a $100 ticket which also required a court appearance.

In court, the judge addressed me because he realized Riquet's English was not up to par. While looking at the police report, and without raising his eyes from the papers, he said "So Renee, tell us why you want to destroy the town of East Hampton". Between sobbing tears I whimpered that I didn't want to destroy East Hampton, it's my husband who doesn't know the difference between inches and centimeters and didn't realize the truck was too high for the bridge. We got off with the $100 fine and the admonition of learning American measurements. I was mortified – though Riquet, not so much, he really didn't understand most of the proceedings.

Marriages

This is a somewhat odd chapter heading but it's probably useful in putting things and events in perspective.

This is a topic I have been avoiding not so much because it may appear painful, but because I have somehow always managed to bury unpleasant experiences and just go forward. I don't dwell, I just try not to repeat the same mistakes. It works, sometimes.

Unfortunately, my first marriage ended in divorce. We were married 13 years and had no children because I had several miscarriages and other similar problems, the last of which landed me in the hospital with a number of life threatening complications that cured me of trying to get something that was obviously not in the books for me.

Unlike the "Never give up" platitude one hears so often, the fact is that sometimes you just have to give up, or go another route. Unfortunately, there was no other route as our marriage simply disintegrated, nothing bad, it just died, like the embryos.

Our divorce was very civilized – everything was split down the middle; I got the Baccarat crystal, the Limoges china, the extensive silverware and other household items including the Gallé lamps while he got all the Napoleonic artifacts and Roman coins and artifacts from his archeological digs, which were worth more than all the dining room tchotchkes that were important to me. I must add that some of the Baccarat sets had a special meaning for me because one set was part of a collection produced for the Vatican in 1970. I was very proud of that acquisition.

The truth is that living in Nancy, there was not much to do on weekends because after visiting the Luneville chateau, there wasn't much else of interest except the town of Baccarat which was a few miles away. So we often drove to Baccarat especially on Sundays when the 3 major factory outlets were open to the public so you could get tons of those crystal products at a reduced price. That's how we got the left over Vatican production.

The only bone of contention was the Electrolux vacuum cleaner – it came with two cats. Whoever got the cats, got the vacuum cleaner. One of the cats, Napoleon, was a very fluffy Persian, and it required industrial strength vacuuming to keep the house from drowning in his fur.

After several days of negotiations, I got the cats, and the Electrolux. We remained friends over the years and I even visited him and his new wife in Texas.

After Riquet and I got divorced and sold the apartment in NY, I bought a studio apartment in another co-op building. This was the first time I had to be interviewed by the board of directors which annoyed me to no end. I wasn't used to it because we didn't have to go through this for our first apartment. That was probably because in the mid-1970's it was just the beginning of the wild conversions from rental to co-op ownership. Now it was some 10 years later, I was in a foul mood for a variety of reasons – the divorce, the hospital tragedies, having to pack and move and being alone. I was basically annoyed at having to start a new life. I wanted to move away from to New York, to New Mexico. Why New Mexico? I have no idea - seemed exotic and as far away from New York as possible. Needless to say, I have never been there but that's my way of rebelling against the status quo, pick something out of the air, like the trip to Ouagadougou.

However, my parents were very much against my moving and I finally gave in stayed in NY and looked for a small apartment. This is how I ended up buying a studio apartment in Murray Hill.

When I heard that I needed to be interviewed by the co-op board to see if I fit in, I just lost it. Being crabby to begin with about this whole move, I found this step of the process degrading and was annoyed beyond all reason.

So when I came for this interview in someone's apartment, I came with an attitude. My attitude deteriorated further at the sight of the board. They were sitting in a number of chairs lined up like a firing squad and my chair was several feet away, facing them. It reminded me of the oral exams in France which also reminded me of firing squads. The fact is that it was more like a scene of an argument in front of the Supreme Court than a firing squad. But what did I know about the justice system here – so I apologize for comparing a scene similar to a Supreme Court hearing to a scene in front of a firing squad.

Enter prospective husband #2 – Sheldon Palmer - he was a member of the firing squad, umm, I mean board of directors. I found out later from him and other board members, that he said to the board president, as soon as I walked in and threw my mink coat nonchalantly on the floor that he was going to marry me! What a guy.

I guess the fact that I was crabby and snippy appealed to him, considering that as a child, his older sister nicknamed him "Ob" (short for "Obnoxious"). He must have felt that he had met his soulmate, another snarky soul. How right he was (and is.)

I guess what actually did it was when they asked me if I had any pets. The usual answer would have been, "I have a dog, a cat, a fish, etc." My answer was just "Yes". This of course elicited the next question, "What kind of pets?" My answer, after a few seconds, was "Don't worry; they'll fit in the elevator".

Now I could see they were getting annoyed, except for prospective husband #2 who was grinning like a Cheshire cat. So to avoid any nasty outbreaks, I volunteered, "2 cats which are still in dispute with my ex-husband since part of the agreement stipulates that whoever gets the cats, gets the Electrolux vacuum cleaner and I really want that vacuum cleaner". What I really wanted to say is that I have a giraffe and a porcupine. But that would have taken it too far.

After I moved into the apartment, prospective husband #2, Shelly, called me one day on the phone. Not ever having been with it regarding the salacious intentions of men, I assumed he was calling to admonish me for some tenant infraction — playing music too loud, cooking something with a foul odor, I don't know – I just assumed it was about some complaint from someone in the building. I was completely taken aback when he asked me what I was doing, and that he was in the bathtub (huh?) and would I go out for a drink with him.

The rest is history, 32 years later and counting.

But one might wonder what exactly attracted me to him? The same thing that I already mentioned about my requirements - the head. On our first date, I found out that he's a lawyer, which kind of turned me off at first – no offense to lawyers, my experiences with this class of people wasn't always felicitous.

But he had an encyclopedic knowledge of the world, art, culture, music, science, and especially history and what really did it was a very simple revelation: he knew the name of ancient Romania, namely Dacia. That did it for me. I never met anyone who knew this, outside of Romania I mean.

Next, he was a chemist, as he was a patent lawyer. I learned that in order to be a patent lawyer, you need to have a science degree. Ok, the chemistry alone was an interesting coincidence but then I found out that he had the same chemistry accident as I had in our barn in Borsa, only 10 years before me. So here we are, 2 people from 2 different continents, having had the same chemistry accident, 10 years apart. How's that for karma?

Finally, the sense of humor was more about wit than silly jokes. One night, while in East Hampton, I woke up in the middle of the night because I heard some noise like fire crackers. I went out to the living room and found Shelly shooting Coke cans on the deck with a BB gun. I asked him what the hell he was doing. He said he was practicing to shoot Nazis in case they tried to invade the Hamptons again. Enough said.

But the best thing about husband #2 is that Shelly, came with 2 adorable children, James & Caroline and 2 cats. My life was complete.

One last point about marriage is my relationship with wedding gowns. This might explain a lot about my personality, though I'm not quite sure what exactly.

For the wedding in France I bought a dress in New York, some white lacy summer thing made in Mexico which I saw in the window of a store somewhere downtown, in the Village.

Unfortunately, my future mother-in-law insisted that according to their customs, the groom's mother has to buy the dress for the bride, so she bought me a non-descript beige dress from a local store that looked nothing like a wedding gown. It was just an ivory knee-length thing, not even a cocktail dress; just a boring ivory dress with long sleeves. But I didn't argue, didn't seem that important.

For my second wedding, I was completely in charge, which is unfortunately an example of why I should not have been in charge.

I bought a dress some 2 weeks before the wedding. Since I worked near the Empire State building, I went to Lord & Taylor during lunch hour to look for a gown. It was amazing that I found one so quickly in the Junior department – in fact that same dress was available in a variety colors, which should have tipped me off that I might have been in the wrong department but seeing the dress in a beautiful crème color, and at only $175, I just grabbed it and was very proud of myself for having found a beautiful wedding gown for such a low price when I knew that some women spent up to $2,000-$3,000 for wedding gowns. I also bought white sandals, in a shoe store across the street, $17.

Figure 10 - The wedding (prom) dress

The only thing I didn't like about the dress is that it was strapless which I thought was not appropriate. It needed to be a bit more demure. So I bought some lace, strung it up on a piece of elastic and created a nice off-the shoulder flounce/valance that I pinned to the dress with two safety pins. Really haute couture!

About a week before the wedding I realized why the dress was so cheap – it was not a wedding gown, it was a prom dress, by Jessica McClintock. I saw it in ad in the New York Times since it was May, therefore just the time to prepare for the prom. I obviously never made it to the bridal department of Lord & Taylor, which I later realized was about 50 feet past the prom section. Oh well, I was in a rush, I had just so much time during my lunch break.

But that was just the beginning of the wedding blunders.

The ceremony and reception took place at the Players Club in Gramercy Park. This club where Shelly was a member, is a beautiful neo-classic building;

it was established by Edwin Booth, a great 19th century actor as a private club for actors and others in the entertainment field as a place for artists to mingle among their own. Unfortunately, he was also the brother of John Wilkes Booth who assassinated Abraham Lincoln. Oh well, it was a beautiful setting nonetheless and the ceremony, under an ambulant huppa with a Jewish star on top, performed by Rabbi Ronald Sobel, took place in front of a painting of Laurence Olivier in some Shakespearean costume. A huppa in front of Laurence Olivier! I thought it was fun, certainly a bit unconventional.

But before I even got to the club, I had a bit of a mishap in the hotel room we rented for the weekend – I cut my leg with a small manicure scissor and was bleeding all over the dress. I spent half an hour in the club's bathroom cleaning the blood off the wedding dress.

I also forgot to get a bouquet, so none of the wedding pictures have me looking like a real bride, except one when a club employee let me hold a small potted plant from the terrace. We also never took typical wedding poses with the family so the pictures look more like a big party than your traditional wedding album.

The final straw was that we somehow forgot to arrange for a car to take us back to the hotel after it was all over so there we were, bride and groom, hailing a taxi on Third Avenue.

So much for my instincts concerning tradition - a total failure. Oh, and no honeymoon, forgot about that too.

But on our 20th anniversary, Shelly said he had something special planned for this celebration. He asked me to put on one of my Chanel suits because we were going to the Metropolitan Museum. Why did I need to wear a Chanel suit to visit a museum? He just smiled. Ok, so we wandered around the museum a bit, had a nice lunch at the restaurant on the premises and then on the way back in the taxi, he said he had to make a stop on Fifth Avenue for few minutes because he needed to pick up some documents from a client. So we got out on 65th Street and walked into some building which I didn't realize was the side entrance of Temple Emmanuel. We went in and, surprise!

There was Rabbi Sobel waiting for us with wine and hors d'oeuvres to gives us a blessing on our 20th anniversary!

It was just beautiful!

Jobs

I HAVE WORKED FOR A total of 50+ years, in a variety of jobs. I have to say that every job I had was a good experience and I learned something from all of them, about society, people and business. After all, it's not just the work you do but also about the people you work with. I also have to say that though I've never had a specific bad experience, I did have some disappointments but the learning was always more valuable than any unfulfilled expectations.

Temp Jobs

Before I graduated from college, I had a variety of temp jobs, usually summer jobs or after school part time jobs. I got fired from a few of them, like the one from the company where my father was the accountant. My father fired me because I melted the coffee pot. I have no idea how one might melt a coffee pot, but apparently I did it and my father said it would be better if I looked for a job elsewhere.

I also got fired from Lerners (the store no longer exists) because I ate lunch at my desk. I was the receptionist at their downtown corporate office. My "office" was a desk on an upper floor in the empty hallway in front of the elevators. It was not a reception area – it was just a desk in a hallway with closed doors to private offices. They wouldn't give me a lunch break so I ordered lunch and ate it at my desk. They said it looked unprofessional to people coming off the elevator to see the receptionist eating at the desk. I guess it looked perfectly professional to have a young girl sit at a desk all alone in a deserted hallway with closed office doors and elevators where I was exposed to any kind of person coming off the elevator in a public building. Oh well.

One summer job from which I was not fired was kind of unusual technically. I simply was not familiar with this "technology". I was an internal mail courier at the Société Générale bank somewhere around Wall Street. My job was to go around every desk on each floor and collect the internal correspondence that was in the upper tray, the OUT box, separate them depending on which employee they were addressed to, and then put them in a pneumatic tube that would be sucked up inside this "aspirator" gizmo and land on the floor to which the tube was addressed.

Then I would go to that floor, open the tube, remove the memos and distribute them on every employee's desk in the IN box tray. It was an OK job, everyone was very nice, I just found the whole tube process a bit weird. Nothing unpleasant, just weird.

I got into a bit of trouble one day because part of my job was also to monitor the front door during certain times of the day. I don't remember if there was also a security guard or not but one day, when I was monitoring the door, I refused entrance to a man I considered scary looking. He was big guy and very scruffy looking with a 2-day old beard. Really did not look like someone who had any business at a French bank on Wall Street. After some employees saw me arguing with the man behind the glass door, they rushed over to the door and opened it explaining to me that this was … the president of the bank. Ouch! He smiled at me with what looked like pity in his eyes, but I guess to make feel better for the blunder, he said, "Pas mal!" Not bad.

Another time when I mistook the big cheese of a company for a low level employee was when I was taking jazz dance lessons at the Alvin Ailey studio with my friend Daisy. Daisy was in the arts so it was normal for her to take such classes. I have no idea what possessed me to do it – probably I was in love with *A Chorus Line* because I saw it about 4 times and the thing is I always loved jazz dance. So one day, while we're in class with our wonderful teacher Nat Horne, I see this very big guy with a broom coming in and out of our studio. I asked the girl next to me why the janitor keeps coming in and out in the middle of our practice. She said, "Ummm, that's not a janitor. It's Mr. Alvin Ailey, he likes to sweep up the studio floors once in a while." Double ouch!

Another summer job that I did not get fired from was at a lingerie company named Top Form. My job title was Receptionist-Model. I don't think this kind of job still exists. What it meant was that I was the switchboard operator all day except when the house model went out to lunch, so I had to replace her. It took me a little while to learn how to operate the switchboard and not make connection mistakes, like connecting the company president with the wife of one of the employees. At that time, telephones in offices could not make direct outgoing calls. The calls had to go through the switchboard - moi, so that I could give the caller an outside line which were these wires that you plugged in to holes in the switchboard. Think of Lily Tomlin as Ernestine the Operator in Laugh-In, the show from the 1970s – that was me, without the snort.

When I filled in for the model during lunch, I had to put on this slip which was the company's big hit product in 1965 – it was a strapless full slip. The innovative part of this was the fact that it was strapless and there was lots of marketing, as I always saw the ads on buses and other public venues. While I was strutting this novel strapless full slip on a makeshift runway (basically a long conference table off the showroom), these bald men with cigars sitting around the table would always pinch my derriere. This was under the guise of feeling the fabric of course, or as they say in Yidish, "toppin de poch". So I suppose part of their job was to give the models a little "knop" while they were "inspecting" the fabric. When I told my father of this, he said "So knop them back!" Well, it was only a summer job so the knopping came to an end in August.

Figure 11 – The sanitation scene

Upon hearing that I had a "modeling" job, a friend of mine who happened to be an aspiring photographer, decided that I could be useful to him in building up his portfolio if I posed for some pictures. I said Ok, of course – always happy to help a friend. He took tons of pictures of me all over the city and I guess he submitted some of them to various agencies. We lost contact after a while but several years later, I heard from a friend that one my pictures was hanging in the office of the Commissioner of Sanitation. I did not wonder why – it was certainly appropriate.

It was also during the time I had this job that I became terrified of subways. Of course, I took the subway to work every morning as I lived in Queens, and the office was on 34th Street in Manhattan. One morning while in the subway during rush hour, I started not feeling well, very dizzy and lightheaded and the next thing I knew, I collapsed on the floor right by the door. As the train came to a stop at the last station in Queens, people just pushed me out of the way with their feet, basically rolling me out onto the subway platform. Stepping over me, as they all ran to catch other trains.

Nobody paid any attention to me except one man who bent down and tried to revive me and then sat me up and started asking me questions like whether I was pregnant or if I suffered from some disease. I said no to both and conceded that maybe it was because I got up late and didn't have breakfast and maybe that's why I became dizzy. He took me out of the train station onto the street and to a coffee shop where he bought me coffee and a bagel or something. He also called my office from a phone booth to tell them that I would be late because of this accident. After he felt that I was OK, he left. In my confusion and general disorientation, I never asked him for his name or contact info so I could thank him for his kindness. But I learned that people will just kick you out of the way if you're in their way.

Since subways were pretty scary places for someone who was afraid of crowds and claustrophobic as I was, I started taking busses even if it made my trips longer. At least I didn't have to worry about someone kicking me out of a car onto the subway tracks.

But my favorite mode of transportation is and has always been - a taxi! And I never had any problems except once with a psycho, the likes of which I seem to attract.

One day I was taking a taxi to go to the Javitz Center on 10th Avenue for some trade show. I got into a taxi near my apartment in Murray Hill and told the driver the address. Everything was OK, until he got to 9th Avenue where he made a left turn on 34th Street instead of a right turn. I asked him where he was going and he said, he was going his way. I didn't understand what that meant so I told him the Javitz Center was in the opposite direction and he needed to turn around. He ignored me. As he came to a stop at a red light by the entrance to the Lincoln Tunnel, I jumped out of the cab. He ran after me and literally dragged me back and said he would turn around.

He did turn around, all the while cursing at me and telling me to go back where I came from – whatever that meant – and basically screaming like a lunatic. He also drove about 50 mph which scared the daylights out of me and I was sure he was going to drive me into the Hudson River. He stopped short at the light on 10th Avenue and I paid him through the small opening in the partition. He slammed the partition lid over my fingers – I shrieked out in pain, I thought he broke my fingers and just got out of the car. My fingers had a big dent and were turning a dark red. Then he did the funniest thing – he threw my money out the passenger window onto the sidewalk.

Well, I was not going to let this pass. I lodged a complaint with the Taxi & Limousine Commission and several weeks later, I was called for the hearing. The driver was there too, represented by a union attorney. I was not represented by anybody but I did bring Shelly along for moral support because frankly, I was still kind of scared of this guy. When I finally saw him face to face, I almost cracked up laughing since I never saw his face except the back of his head during the entire taxi ride.

His hair was in dreadlocks and he was wearing the most gigantic Jewish star on a necklace that I had ever seen. I mean the star was the size of a dessert plate – never seen anything so huge, at least not as a piece of jewelry. The hearing was quite comical because after the judge read aloud my complaint, the response from the lunatic was that I was anti-Semitic and that's why he was upset. When the judge asked him what specifically made him think I was anti-Semitic, he said that I was giving him instructions on how to go to my destination. When the judge asked him what made this anti-Semitic behavior, he said that people like to boss Jews around as if they were slaves. The rants from the driver went on for several minutes as he gave us lectures on how his tribe was the real Jews and others are fakes or something like that.

At this point, my husband couldn't restrain himself anymore; I thought he was going to choke laughing. And so were the judge and the loony's representative. When I told the judge that his accusation was a bit ludicrous since I am Jewish, the nutcase just looked at me and made some kind of grimace. The fact is that here we were, in the judge's chamber, 5 Jews, the judge with a yarmulke and the union rep also Jewish. And this man is insisting that I'm anti-Semitic.

The judge told him that he's not fit to be in a job where he deals with people and that he should look for another occupation. He also got two consecutive 30 days suspensions and was told that he was lucky I was not suing him personally and the TLC for the physical attack in almost breaking my fingers.

What have I done to attract this type of lunatic? Must be some cursed karma.

Fashion Industry Jobs

When I returned to New York from France in September 1972, I had a job offer lined up at a publishing company but it was to start in January, in other words 3 months later. I was to write manuals, mostly for language classes.

Unfortunately, since Riquet was French and therefore had no work papers and was unable to get any kind of job because he couldn't speak English, it was up to me to get a job as soon as possible – mainly to pay the rent.

My parents helped with food and other necessities. Therefore the plan was to get a temporary job until my publishing position became available. So I started looking at the classifieds and lo and behold, I saw a job opening for a receptionist at Christian Dior on 7th Avenue. The description that caught my attention was that it would be helpful if the candidate spoke French. I got the job.

Riquet eventually also got a job as a geography teacher at the Lycée Français.

Christian Dior

After about 2 months working as a receptionist, I got a promotion to Assistant in the Licensing Department mainly because the woman who held that job left for a position at another company. I was now reporting to the Vice President of Licensing, Mary Lee Fletcher. This also included a $10 a week raise, so now I was making a whopping $165 a week. The president of the company in Paris was Jacques Rouet and my job was to send the licensee sales reports to Paris and to act as Mr. Rouet's interpreter when he came to New York to meet with the various licensees.

My boss, Mary Lee, was a bit strange – I actually liked her a lot and I give her credit for teaching me how to write professional and effective memos as well as teaching me what business was all about. What I mean by strange is that she didn't look like someone working in fashion especially at a label like Dior. At least not what I imagined such a person would look like. But what did I know? She dressed in drab nondescript suits, had shoulder length unkempt grayish hair and no make-up. She was somehow mannish, very cut and dry, but very business-like and professional.

Obviously, this was not my environment, since I came from an academic background and the business world was totally foreign to me. So was the executive hierarchy, something I was not familiar with either. Mary Lee was terrified of the Paris management – I guess it was a big deal at that time for a woman to be a Vice President of a company like Dior. Also, she didn't speak French which I guess made her feel somewhat uncomfortable with the Paris crew, which I definitely understood. Mary Lee also had the strangest diet – during the 2 years I was at Dior, Mary Lee ate the same thing at lunch, in the office: 1 small can of shrimp and ketchup. That's it.

I think that was when I learned about WASPs. I never heard that term before but she explained it. They eat very bland foods, they are usually very skinny, and never show any emotion. That's it, that was my introduction to WASPhood. It was interesting but not very exciting. I also learned she was from Locust Valley and that she lived on Beekman Place. I was at her apartment several times – very nice but kind of impersonal, although with lots of books. That's about all I knew of her. As it is probably apparent by now, I never asked personal questions so I didn't know much about her family, such as whether she was single because she was divorced or widowed – nothing. Unless someone offered this kind of info, I was always in the dark about my co-workers or superiors' private lives.

As an aside, the woman who was responsible for bringing Mary Lee her lunch was also the accessories buyer for the company as it was the factory where most of the ready-to-wear was made. Rose was responsible for buying the trimmings - zippers, buttons and other objects required in the manufacturing of garments. One day she was interviewing another woman for a position as her assistant.

That was when I heard one of the most preposterous questions which I later realized was typical of the fashion industry – the kind of minutiae that only fashion people understand. During the interview where she questioned the candidate about her buying experience, she asked her what kind of buttons she bought. The woman replied, as I guess I would have, "All sorts of buttons". That's when Rose asked, "OK, but do you have any experience in buying Blue buttons?" Huh? I never heard the answer because I ran into my office and exploded laughing. Only at Dior!

The interpreter task I performed when Jacques Rouet was in town was a typically sneaky European ruse because Jacques Rouet spoke flawless, if accented English but having an interpreter at these meetings gave him the edge of having the time to formulate an answer while I was translating what the hapless licensee was saying. It was great theater - none of these manufacturers suspected that Rouet understood every word but was playing them for time. Or maybe they did, but felt obligated to indulge him otherwise they might lose the lucrative deal they had in selling Dior products. Besides being an interpreter during Rouet's visits to New York, I was also a general gofer.

Among the various errands I had to run for him, none was stranger than the time he gave me a list of berry flavored douches I was supposed to pick up at a certain drugstore. I did not know what a douche was because "douche" in French means shower so I didn't understand how you could buy a shower, and a strawberry flavored one at that. Apparently, Rouet's second wife, who was Swedish, had rather kinky tastes. That's what I was told by some people in the office when I asked for some clarification about the douche expedition. OK - that was another lesson, so I not only learned about business, I also got a peek into sex. All learning was happily welcomed.

Back to Mary Lee, who was in charge of structuring and managing licensee contracts for Dior. As everyone in the fashion industry knows, licensees are the cash cow of the brand. If the licensing program is successful over the counter, then the license owner, in this case Dior, just sits and collects money as the royalties roll in. This was one of the best learning experiences I had about the fashion industry. It basically set the stage for what was to become a 25 year career in fashion. Needless to say, when the publishing job became available … I passed.

How could I possibly leave a job where a country bumpkin like me, from Transylvania, got to hobnob with the President of Dior, Marc Bohan, the house designer, Phillippe Guibourget, the designer of the Miss Dior label, meetings at Diana Vreeland's apartment, and other highfalutin characters that I did not know even existed. Plus, I was learning about the world of business which was such a novelty.

For example, one thing I learned was how to destroy a brand. Because that's exactly what Christian Dior did back in the early 70s. They destroyed their brand through pure greed by licensing the name helter skelter to any manufacturer that wanted to produce merchandise under that label with no quality or design control. I assume that neither the Dior couture wasn't doing that well nor the Miss Dior ready-to-wear so licensing was an easy way to get revenue if you had a well-known brand name. So you could buy a Dior blouse in some discount stores in the US for $24. About the only thing they didn't license was toilet paper, like Pierre Cardin did. There were so many licensees, that it took two full pages of licensee lines in those green ledgers we used to maintain to track royalties. That was my job, to keep a ledger of all the licensee sales and send them to Paris so the office knew what royalties to expect.

One entertaining moment I remember was when we received a letter from a customer somewhere in Florida. He explained that he bought a Dior shirt at some local store and that when he got home, he noticed that the shirt had 7 buttons but only 6 button holes and therefore asked if we could send him an extra button hole. Ok, so some Dior licensees made crappy products, but at least the customers had a sense of humor. They sent him a new shirt, I assume with an equal number of buttons and button holes, though the original extra button was probably a replacement in case he lost one.

Now, my job paid $175 a week (I got another $10 raise after 1 year), so even in 1972-1974, that was a crummy salary. Needless to say, on that salary, I could not afford to buy nice clothes. The rent on my apartment in Queens was $250 and between all our other expenses and travel, there was barely any money left. So I shopped at Lerners, Mays and Macy's in the Junior departments.

Imagine my dismay, when my boss started to complain that my clothes looked cheap and not reflective of the luxury company I was working for. Since our office was in the same place as the factory where the Dior ready-to-wear was being made, I asked my boss whether I could get a small clothing allowance – like a skirt one season, a blouse the next season – just so that I could start to build a little wardrobe. The answer was no because only the showroom sales person, Marie B, was entitled to a clothing allowance since she had to sell the collection to buyers from stores like Saks Fifth Avenue, Bergdorf Goodman, Neiman Marcus, etc., and of course she had to look good, wearing the company's merchandise.

Okay, well, then I asked, could I get a raise (after 2 years)? The person whom I replaced in this position 2 years earlier was making $200 a week and I was still making only $175 after almost 2 years. So my boss asked Paris for permission to give me a raise. The answer was positively extraordinary: "Please explain to Renee that we do not work at Dior for money, we work for the glory of Dior". Ooookay!

The truth was that in Paris couture houses, at least at that time, much like at glamorous companies in the US, many of the young "employees" were socialites who were "working" at Dior or other couture houses for almost no pay – it was just something to put on their resume before they got married to some count, marquis or other entitled master of the universe. And they got free clothes because, like celebrities today, they traveled in circles that were Dior's customers. Nothing wrong with that. Unfortunately, my father was not a duke, and my husband was a teacher at a French school in New York. So when I went shopping for food, I had to produce dollars at the cash register. They simply would not accept any Dior glory for that breast of chicken. So I started looking for a new job and then managed to get myself fired in a most spectacular performance.

I may have been naïve about business and abused as an employee but having lived in France and acting as Rouet's foil, gave one a certain sense of the duplicity and manipulative nature of man. Just look at how Rouet played his US associates. The truth is that European history is full of spectacular duplicitous acts like poisonings, back stabbings, treason and other charming human endeavors. By comparison, the only scandal I ever heard about in American history was the Boston Tea Party and an assassination or two. How banal. I also learned that revenge is a dish best served cold, an expression that comes from – who else, but a French writer, Laclos in the book *Les Liaisons Dangereuses* – the ultimate narrative about duplicity and treason. So I plotted my departure as a big French bang. The conditions were actually in my favor at that time because of the position of Dior in the fashion arena.

At that time, the absolute hottest designer was Yves St. Laurent. Not only was Dior a fading brand compared to St. Laurent, but to add insult to injury, Dior never got over the fact that St. Laurent, who used to work for Dior, after Christian Dior passed away, left the house to start his own label, and now was the darling of the fashion world. The jealousy and resentment was enormous. You couldn't even mention St. Laurent's name around the office, it was like mentioning Voldemort in a Harry Potter movie. St. Laurent's couture and ready-to-wear were on every cover of every fashion magazine, and St. Laurent himself was a big celebrity what with his entourage of socialites like Loulou de la Falaise, Betty Catroux and others, while Dior's designer, Marc Bohan barely got any "personality" press and you almost never saw any Dior couture or ready-to-wear in the fashion magazines. I don't know whether Dior understood at the time that one reason they had no fashion credibility was because you could buy a "Dior" blouse for $24 in some of the junkiest stores in the country. Not exactly a message of exclusivity.

So I went to St. Laurent and asked if there were any job openings – anything. Yes there was a job opening in the PR department, as an assistant to the PR director, Marina S. I got the job and asked if it would be OK to give my current employer 3 weeks' notice. They agreed.

Now, at the same time, Dior had a big event coming up that week – the annual licensee party, usually in a midtown restaurant with all the French management in attendance as well as about 200 licensees. I dreaded this because I didn't have anything appropriate to wear at this big event especially since as the Licensee assistant it was my job to greet everyone at the door while my bosses complained that my clothes looked cheap. So I was really depressed - they didn't want to give me a raise so I could afford to buy some new clothes, and they didn't want to give me a blouse or something from the production that was being done right under my nose, so how was I to look elegant at this affair?

By then, I wasn't only depressed at my lowly rank but angry that they put me in this position. So I did the unthinkable: I blew almost 2 months' salary plus some extra $$$ from my parents on the ultimate St. Laurent outfit that was in every magazine that season. It was a flower print silk skirt and a matching twin set in Black with stripe details matching the skirt colors; a very cute outfit. In fact, it's the outfit I wore to the St. Laurent interview the previous week which obviously worked in my favor.

Figure 12 – The famous YSL outfit that got me fired from Dior; in Paris with Barbara Lauder from Coach Leatherware

So there I am at this big Christian Dior event, with all the Dior management in attendance, all the US Dior licensees and I was wearing the most publicized St. Laurent outfit of the season! The reaction was pure shock!

I was fired immediately the following day with 2 weeks' severance pay. Woohoo! So I had a 2 week vacation before I started the St. Laurent job. It was one of the best, most satisfying plans I had ever made. I guess I had an instinct for the French business style.

YVES SAINT LAURENT

I may have left Dior with a bang but at St. Laurent, the departing bang was literal. I was lucky I wasn't sued for destruction of property. My stint at St. Laurent was kind of short – I believe less than a year. I worked as an assistant, secretary, gofer for Marina who was the Publicity Director or something like that for Yves St. Laurent. Her office was a Park Avenue apartment on 60th Street where one of the bedrooms was transformed into an office. I was the only employee. Frankly, I think that was a temporary job because she really didn't need an assistant after the major event that I was hired for had ended.

The event was a fashion show at the Pierre Hotel presented by none other than Monsieur St. Laurent himself. That had never been done before so it was a big thing. My job was to make sure the invitations were sent out correctly and to handle phone calls from the press and others. The reception committee was a who's who of New York society at the time led by the Duchess of Windsor though I don't think she ever showed up.

The funny thing for me, as a newbie in the fashion industry, was that I never understood the brouhaha surrounding fashion designers. They really didn't mean anything to me and especially with respect to St. Laurent; I could not personally appreciate the aura surrounding him. I had a St. Laurent pea coat when I lived in France and was in the academic field; all my friends had one, it was just a great all-weather coat, obviously quite affordable so it was all about the comfort and novelty of the design rather than the label. All clothing in France was of excellent quality, compared to some of the junk I used to get at department stores in New York.

During the setup at the Pierre where the ballroom was decorated like a tent with yards and yards of silk draped over the ceiling and other decorative items I simply can't recall, I got to meet the French team - Yves St. Laurent, Pierre Berge, Moujik (the dog), and Loulou de la Falaise.

Yves was very sweet and warm though kind of timid. Pierre Bergé came out with the dog Moujik who howled at me but luckily didn't bite. He was also very polite and rather charming. But the one I liked the best was Loulou de la Falaise who climbed up on a piano and lay down on it while watching all the preparations. I found her very entertaining and amusing - a real character.

The show was great and was covered by every fashion publication. In fact, even my name was mentioned in several out of town newspapers before the event since I had to deal with all the calls from editors who wanted to attend. My coverage was not very pleasant; I was described as a haughty socialite with a French accent. Aside from the fact that I was very clearly a secretary, since I answered the phones, I didn't know where the socialite portrayal came from, and I do not have, nor have I ever had, a French accent. They actually quoted my responses (falsely) with misspelled words to imitate a French accent. I say the quotes were false because I was reading from a script and the quotes were completely different from what I actually said. They obviously had to enhance my actual comments to make the story more appealing or scandalous to their readers. Whatever! I just laughed.

I suppose they were just unhappy that I could not give positive answers to their requests. This experience and several other encounters with the press have taught me that you can't believe anything you read in the paper. Hmmmm! That sounds very familiar; almost like the disinformation we were accustomed to receiving in Romania. So much for the free press: definitely free but also definitely creative - designed more for entertainment rather than factual reporting. Unfortunately, my employment at St. Laurent did not last long.

Marina was a bit strange but maybe it was me who just didn't understand high society and some of the liberties that come with an elevated life style. Francoise de la Renta (the first wife of Oscar de la Renta) was there every other day as her decorator and she did a really nice job by acquiring interesting furniture and accessories for the apartment. But one day, as I met her in the elevator, she kissed me, which I guess was OK though I was not her equal in any sense because of the disparity of our social standing. But then she also touched me in a way that creeped me out, but I didn't say anything to anybody. I just ran out of the elevator and locked myself in my office. After that, whenever she came in, if Marina was not home, I would make some excuse for having to go out on an errand.

Another time, when I came back from lunch I found Marina in a somewhat compromising position with another woman, Frances X, a designer for Tiffany. When I mentioned this to some friends who worked at the headquarters of a company that represented several French design firms, I was told that this was nothing new, that everybody knew that she had an on and off relationship with Francoise Sagan, the author of *Bonjour Tristesse*. Francoise Sagan was well known for playing on both teams. Ok, who cares what she did in her private life? I do know she was very much loved by Yves, and that she had very loving and artistic framed letters from him on the fireplace mantel. One I remember had a color drawing of a snake around the top of the paper.

And there were also some amusing moments, like when she got visits from the Andy Warhol team with whom she was very close. Bob Colacello used to call daily and one day this man came in and told me his name was something Smith and that he had an appointment with Marina. He was wearing dark glasses and a hat with a huge brim. I said, "She's in the living room Mr. Warhol" to which he responded, "I guess it didn't work". Well, who could disregard that blond hair?

Of all the jobs I had in my twenties, that was both the most interesting and most unprofessional atmosphere. First of all, the fact that the office was in her apartment and I was mostly all alone was very isolating and depressing. Also, many times when I arrived in the morning, the apartment looked like there had been a party the night before, with dirty dishes in the sink, food items all over the stove and floor – a real mess. The fact is that after that big fashion show event, there was really nothing much for me to do so I was really bored.

Although there were no rules at the time about proper behavior in a work environment, there were several comments Marina made that I found offensive. The last straw was when we were talking about something innocuous, which I don't even remember, but I mentioned something about an expense I had and that I had to withdraw money from my savings account. To which she replied "You're so Jewish, only Jews have savings accounts". At that point I just had enough. I got up and left by slamming the door, which broke the glass above the wooden frame. The next day I told her accountant that I'd be happy to pay for the broken glass but that I was not coming back, to which he replied that it was not necessary, and that I was fired. So then I had the nerve to ask, "Do I get severance pay?" To which he answered, "Goodbye Renee, be well". Hmmm, I really screwed that one up.

Coach Leatherware

After St. Laurent I got a job with Coach Leatherware as the assistant to the president, Miles Cahn, which was a glorified secretarial position but a lot of fun. At that time Coach was a family business owned by Miles & Lillian Cahn, two of the nicest people I ever met, as people and employers.

Besides the typical secretarial tasks, I was involved in whatever Miles was working on, PR, advertising, marketing, anything.

One experience that stands out was the incredible popularity of the Coach brand at that time. This was way before American consumers became obsessed with designer labels.

Figure 13 - at Coach Leatherware showroom, wearing a Dior jacket

The Coach customers were absolutely in love with all the Coach products, all around the country. At that time, the only advertising Coach did was small ads in The New Yorker magazine - that's all. Why people in the mid-west and all over the country were reading The New Yorker was something I never quite understood but the popularity of Coach handbags was extraordinary because of one factor which I have never again seen in any other company I worked for in the fashion industry. Coach used to receive an average of 50 LOVE letters a week from customers all over the country. It was mind boggling. In all these letters, they also asked for the brochure we used to print listing all the stores that carried Coach products. Some people wrote that they traveled 200 miles to some store across the state line to buy a Coach bag. At that time all Coach bags were made of glove leather, the same leather used in baseball gloves. Therefore it was real cowhide and since they were unlined, you could see that it was real leather – the inside was rawhide. One aspect of the design of the bags I always loved was the legend stamped inside – Made in New York City!

At one point, the Coach management decided to launch some larger ads in addition to the small one column ads in the New Yorker. The ad agency came up with a number of full page ads in various newspapers. However, somebody apparently did not do a good job of proofreading one of the ads because lo and behold, there was this huge ad that promoted Coach bags made of "bridal leather" instead of "bridle leather". Ouch! We got letters and letters – some hysterically funny, some expressing offense that we would promote leather made of the skin of brides. Huh? Some people are just dumber than doorknobs.

A little aside about the history of Coach bags. Anyone can find references to the history of Coach, so I don't know whether this little anecdote is known. The Cahns gave me a lot of information about the company, so I knew that it started out as a manufacturer of men's wallets in the early 1940s. The switch to bags came sometime in the 1960s after several incidents involving spilled chicken soup being carried in paper shopping bags that Mrs. Cahn's mother used to carry to the Cahn family on the upper West Side. That's when Lillian suggested to her husband that he make a leather shopping bag so that her mother could safely carry the soup without spilling it and tearing the paper bag. That was the beginning. It started with a shopping bag to carry chicken soup. How much sweeter can this get?

I spent several fabulous years at Coach during which time I helped with the setup of their first outlet store in Amagansett with their daughter Julie. For the non-New Yorkers among you, Amagansett is a hamlet between East Hampton and Montauk. Until then I had never been in retail, so even setting up a store was a bit of a challenge. Since this was an outlet store for slightly damaged items, like a minor scratch here and there, a little stain, all minor defects that would soon disappear because as you used the bags and wallets, the leather would burnish and turn shiny almost like patent leather or box calf. Everybody who had Coach bags knew this but obviously they couldn't ship goods with even the most minor imperfections to stores like Saks, Bloomingdale's and others. The company rented one of the "stables" at Amagansett Square for the ridiculous sum of $400 for 3 summer months. Ah, the good old days! Julie and I arrived on a Saturday morning in early

June with a truck to set up the store. This included not only the merchandise but also the shelving and other store fixtures. A couple of employees from the company helped with the installation of the fixtures while Julie and I set up the merchandise.

This took almost an entire day, and people hanging out on the lawn between the barn stores and the Royal Fish restaurant, were constantly knocking on the door to ask when the store would open. We finally opened the doors around 8:30pm. It is impossible to describe the frenzy – it was like one of those commercials for Black Friday. Within 1 hour the entire store was emptied and we had to shut the doors because there was nothing left to sell. The store was closed for about 3-4 days until we were able to gather more "imperfect" products which we did not have. So we began to thoroughly inspect all the stock; we became fussier and more discerning by scrutinizing this perfectly good merchandise to find even the most microscopic barely visible imperfection. It was a tough job keeping inventory for the outlet store in Amagansett.

A side note about the Royal Fish restaurant which is long gone but which at that time, in the mid -70s was a really nice place to hang out. It was one of Lauren Bacall's favorite places. You could always hear her howling with laughter at the bar.

There were 5 stores in those barns at the time – an ice cream store, Le Sportsac, Julie's personal store named Colors, Coach Leatherware and a store owned by my good friend Ursula who at that time was a stewardess at Pan Am (of course, now she would be a flight attendant) and opened the store with wonderful merchandise from Europe. We all used to hang out at the ice cream store with people like Joseph Heller whom of course I didn't know because I knew nothing about American literature. I was told he wrote *Catch-22* which I confused with *Catcher in the Rye* since it was one of those books I had to read in high school when I couldn't speak a word of English. Of course, I mortified myself one day when I was sitting next to him licking an ice cream and wanted to make some conversation and I told him that I really enjoyed *Catcher in the Rye*. I stayed away from the ice cream store for the rest of the season. A few years later, the Coach store moved to different locations in Amagansett and then to East Hampton.

As this was their first venture into retail, the Cahns now set their eyes on a bit more company owned retail such as an outlet store in Vermont and then, wonder of wonders – a store in Paris.

But first Vermont. This was the sort of goofy experience that can only happen in a federal republic like the United States because it's related to geography and the fact that different states can have the same town names as other states. Forget about Rome, NY or Paris, Arkansas, Paris, Idaho and more half a dozen other American cities named Paris, such as Paris, NY. That's weird enough.

But when two such identically named cities are close to each other in neighboring states, and you don't have a GPS in the car because they didn't exist in the early 1970s, and you're driving at night after a full day's work on the I-95 to Burlington, Vermont, it's very easy to take a wrong turn off the highway following a sign that does not indicate the state you're in and end up in …. Burlington, Maine. That's because Burlington Maine was closer than Burlington, Vermont. So by 3AM, we realized that while we were in fact in Burlington, we were in Burlington, Maine, not Burlington Vermont. Chalk that one to an endless spirit of adventure and disregard of details.

Fortunately the store opening did not depend on our immediate presence because it took us 6 hrs to get to Vermont. The good thing about getting older is that you don't just jump into adventures without some advance planning or some basic thinking. That's just what I didn't do when I was young - I just jumped into things and took off. Who cared where I landed? Obviously, not me.

That's how I once boarded a flight to Mecca instead of New York at the recently opened Charles De Gaulle airport with those circular stairways before the gates that all looked the same. That gate was next to the New York gate but did I look? Of course not. Since at that time, in the mid 70s they were not as rigorous as today in boarding flights, nobody looked at my boarding pass until I got on the plane, and I was even shown to my seat. It's only when I noticed that all the passengers were wearing Arab attire, which was kind of strange for a flight to New York, I asked the flight attendant if this was the flight to New York. That's when she actually looked at my boarding pass and cracked up laughing. I was lucky I didn't miss the flight at the next gate.

So after Burlington, it was the store in Paris. Ah, who could have been happier than I to set up a retail store in Paris – right? Though I didn't know anything about the retail business in France, and frankly neither did the Cahns, they befriended a woman who had a store on Rue Mazarine, on the Left Bank, who agreed to carry Coach bags.

I don't really remember how the store in Rue Mazarine did but a year later, the Cahns decided to open their own store on Rue Jacob and I was sent to get the paperwork done and hire the staff. Setting up the company was not an easy task. The paper work, all in French, was rather daunting not to mention the exorbitant fees – no wonder it's so hard to set up shop in France. The taxes are crippling. But it eventually got done. The store was opened and did rather well considering that this was not a well known brand in Paris.

Figure 94 - Coach Leatherware on Rue Mazarine, Paris

During the time I spent in Paris setting up the store, I also got friendly with the owner of the art gallery across the street which was at the intersection of Rue Jacob and Rue Bonaparte where I had friends who lived in one of those majestic townhouses. The gallery was owned by Dina Vierny who I learned was Maillol's model and also posed for Matisse and other artists. But what was even more interesting to me was that she was Jewish, and was born in our area, Chişinău, Bessarabia but left for France with her parents many years before the war. I later learned that she was also in the Resistance in the South of France during the war.

Figure 15 – The Day The Stole the Mona Lisa

One other interesting experience during my time at Coach was an assignment I got from a friend of the owners. The friend, Seymour Reit, was writing a book about the theft of the Mona Lisa in 1911 and needed translations of the French police documents from that time. I translated the documents which became part of the story and he gave me credit in the preface of the book, *The Day They Stole the Mona Lisa* – by Seymour Reit. That was really an enjoyable assignment – the police reports were comical which coincided with my impression of the French police. I don't know why - they always amused me. Well, maybe because I always had good and amusing experiences with the French police.

Before I left Coach Leatherware, the Cahns were very kind in giving me a going-away present: a leather sculpture from the Coach art gallery which was filled with the most incredible art work all made out of leather. I couldn't decide which one I liked most, they were all extraordinary. So I finally picked a leather torso by an artist named Pip Taillefer. It was a mold of his wife's torso, from the back made using a complicated method with plaster mold and heated leather that when cooled shrunk down to this beautiful shining piece of leather sculpture. This sculpture was on my wall for about 30 years until I was contacted by one of the artist's family and returned it to them. It is now living a lovely family life in Oregon along with Pip's other art work.

Figure 106 – Pip Taillefer sculpture

After a few years, I moved to another company, George Rech. This was another French fashion company that opened a retail store on Madison Avenue where the Hermès store is now located. I was the Assistant Manager.

This job turned into a complete disaster after several burglaries where I was awakened by the police several times in the middle of the night to go to the store and assess the damage. I also thought the store manager was a bit strange when we did the day's cash register at the end of the day – we used to sit at the desk in the back office going over the receipts to match them against the cash register tape and there would always be hundred dollar bills falling off her lap which she would explain away as being for a purchase she hadn't yet entered on the register. OK. She was the manager and it was none of my business that she was sloppy.

I decided to leave because I really wasn't comfortable with all the burglaries and I had another job offer – back to Coach, which was very exciting. The Cahns asked me if I would go to Paris for a couple of weeks to take over the store manager's job while she was in the hospital for some back injury. I was to live in her house and also take care of her 3 cats. Was this paradise or what? I packed in a flash and off I flew to Paris.

The second or third day in Paris, I ended up in a hospital emergency room because I fell down unconscious in her bedroom. Why? Because the apartment was very strange. It was originally a carriage house and stable. Therefore, on the main floor was the living room, 2-3 steps above was the kitchen, and then, where the hay loft used to be, about 25 feet above the living room, there was some sort of sitting room, the bedroom and bathroom.

Of course, the roof of this whole structure was a mansard which means that the ceiling from the bedroom to the bathroom was at a sharp angle which came down to the floor in the bathroom. To get into the bathtub, you had to slide in horizontally. So of course, in the middle of the night, I got up to go to the bathroom and forgot to bend down before going through the bathroom door where the ceiling beam was about 4 ½ feet high. I banged my head against the beam and fell flat on my back. I woke up around 6AM with a horrific headache so I immediately went to the hospital where they told me I'd be OK; it was just a little bump on my forehead. Otherwise my stay in Paris was a lot of fun while managing the Coach store on Rue Jacob. And of course hanging out a lot at Dina Vierny's gallery.

During that time, I also visited the George Rech headquarters to chat with the gentleman who hired me in NY to explain why I had left the job. I found out that after I left that job, the NY store manager was arrested for grand larceny but since she paid back all the money they didn't press charges. Guess it was more than a few hundred dollar bills falling off her lap.

While I was in Paris, I was contacted by a friend from New York who told me that I might be interested in a job when I got back to New York and that company's president was also in Paris for a few days and that maybe I would like to meet him. She told me his name was Richard Bienen. It sounded somewhat familiar but at the time I couldn't place it. Well, of course I said yes – after all, who passes up a job interview especially in Paris? At least I knew it couldn't be in some office in a skyscraper.

Oh, did I forget to mention that I once had a job interview at some T-shirt manufacturing company whose showroom was on the 65th floor of the Empire State Building? Yeah, well that didn't turn out so well because I almost fainted when I got out of the elevator. I went in, sweating, shaking and with my heart beating like a drum and told the receptionist that I was there for the job interview but that I had to sit down for a while because I wasn't feeling well. She brought me a glass of water and while I tried to calm my nerves, the person who was going to interview me came out and asked me if I was OK. I said I would be OK as soon as I got back on the ground and apologized profusely.

I told him that I couldn't go through with the interview because I obviously had some breathing issues at this height, and didn't want to waste his time. He was somewhat amused because I guess the greenish cast of my skin supported my statement. He was extremely kind and offered to take the elevator down with me to make sure that I was alright. I thanked him but I said

I'd be OK. Unfortunately, at that time there was no restaurant with alcoholic drinks on the ground floor, otherwise I would have been in there in a flash to gulp down a double bourbon on the rocks. I may live in a city of skyscrapers but I can't go into one above the 30th floor – I get palpitations. When I look out the window, I need to see people in the street as people, not ants. I'm not afraid of heights outdoors, just not inside a building. Go figure.

Halston Handbags

Anyway, the interview in Paris at the restaurant in Richard's hotel, the Lancaster, was for a job at Halston Handbags. The position was showroom sales at the Halston handbag licensee company and I was to replace someone who was leaving. I accepted in a flash.

After my stint in Paris was over, I flew back to New York and started at the handbag company which was on East 33rd Street. It was across the street from the Empire State Building – yeah. I was definitely happy to be on the other side of the street. As soon as I started working there I asked one of my new colleagues why the name Bienen was kind of familiar. No wonder – Richard Bienen's father had a well-known handbag company several years before that was named Bienen Davis. OK, one mystery solved.

This was a typical showroom sales position, so my job as well as that of my colleagues consisted of working with the designer on creating a collection of handbags and belts, doing presentations of the collection to store buyers in the showroom, filling out the order forms and then back in the office following up with stores who did not send in their orders. That was the crux of it and it was a pleasant atmosphere. I think the only thing that annoyed me was me. It happened several times, after which I told my boss that I wasn't going to do it again, and while he laughed, he agreed, unless it was an emergency. What was it? It was the same thing I encountered with taxi drivers. When I would do a presentation to a group of buyers showing them the collection and explaining the various details, after listening to me attentively, I would always ask at the end, "Well, do you have any question?" "Before you write the order", I'm thinking. What was always the first question? "Where are you from?" This meant that we wasted at least ten minutes discussing my "provenance". This is why I usually stayed hidden unless I was the only one available in the event there was an unscheduled visit from a store buyer.

Like all the other jobs I had before, this was a family business and therefore we were often privy to personal family issues which were sometimes comical, sometimes sad or silly but always perfect grist for the water cooler gossip mill. I never participated much in these exchanges, I guess because I was always a bit of a loner, and other people's issues were always far from my universe, unless I was directly asked to comment.

When I first went to the Halston headquarters in the Olympic Towers, I felt a bit like I was on some kind of spaceship. It wasn't so much the reception area which adjoined the runway where the shows took place, but the wall to wall red carpeting, huge floor to ceiling windows and people who walked around silently, all dressed in Black — head to toe — like aliens.

But hey, I was in the fashion business so I was used to wacko environments. When I first asked the receptionist if Mr. Halston was in the office, just out of curiosity since my meeting was with one of the accessory designers, I was told that he never came in before 2:00 PM. That kind of made me very jealous since I'm not an early morning riser. When I asked why he came in so late, she said that it's because he has to sleep off the night before which he spent at Studio 54. Well, of course that made perfect sense.

Anyway, I think I had only one or 2 meetings there where Mr. Halston was present and he was quite pleasant, distant, but pleasant. But during the fashion shows, he obviously needed more than sleep to keep him awake because after the show, when he came out to take a bow in front of the audience, I noticed white powder under his nose and on his lips, which he kept wiping. Country bumpkin that I was even then, I had to ask my boss what that stuff was on his face. Richard looked at me as though I had just crawled out from under a rock and said "It's his medication". Right. The kind of medication you snort.

Back at the handbag office, I had a couple of entertaining experiences, but first, this one since it's indicative of how much out of "it" I always was.

One day, during Market Week, a colleague and I went to have lunch at a recently opened restaurant in the neighborhood, La Coupole, which was of course a copy of the Parisian brasserie. Market Week, which for those unfamiliar with the fashion industry, is when all the store buyers from across the country come to the New York showrooms to view the collections and place orders for their stores. In recent years it has been renamed Fashion Week, I suppose to give it a more glamorous aura but it's basically the same thing – manufacturers put on a show for the media and prospective store buyers. This is usually twice a year, Spring and Fall and in some product categories, it's 4 times a year.

Anyway, while I was waiting for my friend who was in the ladies room as we were leaving, I noticed that next to our table were 4 gentlemen, one of whom I recognized as the very good looking buyer from the Denver Dry Goods store. Since I'd seen him in the showroom the week before, I said to him, "Nice to see you again Robert, how long are you staying in NY?" to which he replied, "I'm probably leaving tomorrow". So I said, "Well, have a good trip, see you in a few months". To which he replied, "For sure".

At this point, my friend came out of the ladies room and as we started toward the door, she stopped for a split second to look at that table and then told me on the way out, "Did you see who was at that table next to us?". I said, "Of course, it was the buyer from Denver, I said hello to him". To which she replied, "You idiot, that wasn't the buyer from Denver, it's Michael Douglas". Shocked, I went back and took a quick discreet look, and she was right, it was Michael Douglas. Oh well, so I confused two good looking men, so what? At least, he was very pleasant and went along with the charade probably thinking I was some lunatic from another planet. Actually, it proved he was a good actor.

Speaking of actors, the best memory I have from working at the Halston handbag company was an encounter that I don't think any of us will ever forget, if all of us still have the photos. I certainly do. Richard Bienen had a lot of friends in the entertainment business, especially in Hollywood and many of them used to come to the showroom for either a visit or to buy a handbag and they would just hang around and yack. But before I even get to that I must mention another hysterical event that had us in stitches for quite a while. Shopping wholesale is very common in New York since we have the Garment Center where everybody knows someone in the industry who can get them to shop in the showroom instead of paying retail in a store.

Before Christmas, we always had "friends of the house" come in to buy Christmas presents. One day I got a call from Leona Helmsley's office advising us that Mrs. Helmsley would like to make an appointment to see some bags she would like to buy. I told the caller that she could come in any time between 9 and 5 because there was always someone to help. The person insisted that she wanted to have a confirmed appointment. OK, I asked her when Mrs. Helmsley would like to come and confirmed the time and date. The day of the appointment, Mrs. Helmsley arrived with 2 bodyguards.

I come out to the reception desk to greet her and bring her into the showroom. I loved what she was wearing – a snake coat (never seen one of those) and a tight red dress, very flattering, and some very large gold pendant.

After all the greetings and offerings of water, soda, coffee, etc., she asked me if Richard Bienen was around because she wanted to say hello to him. I said that I would check to see if he was available. I went into Richard's office and told him that Leona Helmsley was here and that she wanted to say hello to him. I don't know what he was so busy with but he seemed annoyed because he just didn't have the time for this. Richard was definitely not a celebrity hound, he traveled in such elevated circles in NY and Hollywood that I don't think he would have been much impressed if the President of US popped in the showroom. I managed to persuade him anyway to come out and say hello to her.

So he came out of his office, with a big smile on his face, he certainly knew how to be extremely cordial, and wanted to shake her hand. She put her hands on his shoulders and said, "Richard, you don't remember me?" Richard, of course, looked a little confused and I could see that he was trying to place her. I mean he knew she was Leona Helmsley, but she seemed to insinuate a much older relationship. As he mumbled something, she said "I'm Leona Roberts, remember? I used to work for you and you fired me because I asked you for a raise. That's when I went into real estate." Richard turned a cute shade of pink and I thought his hair would rise up on his head, he was so embarrassed, but then it was endless kissing and hugging and all sorts of reminiscing. She ended up buying 10 handbags for her staff and they made a date to meet sometime in the near future. I guess it pays to keep track of your former employees, you never know when they end up owning the world. Oh well, that was one for several dinner party conversations.

But the real shocker occurred one day when we heard a loud commotion in the reception area. It seemed like all 3 elevators emptied a crowd of people in front of the reception desk. In fact all 3 elevators stopped at our floor and it was full of people stretching their necks until we realized who stepped out of one of the elevators: Cary Grant and his wife Barbara Harris!

I don't have to mention the near riot that ensued in the office as we ran to tell Richard that Cary Grant was here. Well, apparently Richard knew Cary Grant too. Mr. and Mrs. Grant spent some time in the showroom with all of us and indulged us all with all our crazy questions and fawning all over him. They couldn't have been more charming and gracious. He even indulged me when I asked him if he would utter my name as in his famous "Judy, Judy,

Judy" routine which he did – "Renee, Renee, Renee." What a pity that I didn't think of recording it.

Figure 17 - With Cary Grant, his wife Barbara Harris and the Halston Accessories team

We subsequently learned from Richard that Cary Grant was on the board of Faberge and that he came to New York quite often. He also told me several months later that after a visit to Mr. Grant's house in Los Angeles, he showed Richard the framed picture I took of him and his wife with my Polaroid – he kept the picture in their bedroom. This was news, of all the photos of him in the world, he framed a picture from my Polaroid? Whatever, I adored Cary Grant.

One last episode that I remember at this job was a case of sexual harassment that was kind of amusing, at least for me. Although I encountered a lot of this in my work, I never really paid much attention to them. I used to respond in much the same way they talked to me so it always ended up with the bullies retreating with their tails between their legs.

This time though, I got physical, because the guy used to paw me constantly. I took my father's advice from years before of "knopping" back at the cigar smoking bald "shmata business" guys in the lingerie company.

So one day, when this guy was pawing me again while I was sitting at my desk, I got up, grabbed him by his family jewels and told him that if he ever touched me again, I would make an omelet. That ended it and we remained friendly co-workers, though I think he always looked over his shoulder when I was behind him, I guess he felt I was serious about me scrambling and cooking his eggs.

Mark Cross

One of the most entertaining jobs I had was at Mark Cross, in the 1980s. The history of the Mark Cross company is extraordinary in that it started in 1845 making saddles. This was a detail that ultimately figured in my next job.

The saddle maker Mark Cross, sold the company at the turn of the 20th century to an employee, Patrick Murphy who subsequently left it to his son, Gerald Murphy. By then, as cars were replacing horses, and saddles were less and less in demand, the company started diversifying and buying leather goods in Europe to be sold in its store in New York.

Gerald and his wife Sara were friends with, and part of the Jazz Age set, like F. Scott Fitzgerald, Ernest Hemingway and other Americans who spent summers on the Riviera. Gerald Murphy was a colorful character and we had many pictures of him, entering the Mark Cross store in splendid 1920s attire, black cape, hat and all. Descendants of the Murphys are still around, in East Hampton.

At the time I joined the company, it was run by the Wasserberger brothers, Edward and George but was owned by the A.T. Cross pen company. Though the brothers had previously owned the company for over 20 years, they once sold it to another company, then bought it back and then sold it again to A.T. Cross. This last sale happened because of the gold crisis in the early 1980s.

A.T. Cross was renowned for its fountain pens; and since the fountain pen tips were made of a gold alloy, A.T. Cross was becoming concerned that the rising gold prices would affect the pen business. Therefore, the strategy was to diversify their production with other products, not dependent on gold, and which could be manufactured under the same rigorous precision of instrument manufacturing as pens. So they came up with clocks and watches. Not a bad idea except for the fact that they ran into a trademark problem – Mark Cross was also selling watches and they owned the trademark "Mark Cross" for timepieces which obviously would have led to confusion with the A.T. Cross watches. Instead of falling into a quagmire of litigation, A.T. Cross offered to buy the Mark Cross company and thereby acquire all the trademarks, also including the luggage, handbags and other accessories that carried the Mark Cross trademark. I don't need to go into the business details of why this arrangement didn't last very long because even if one doesn't know anything about the difference between making pens and making handbags, the first thing that would jump out at you was the different raw materials – metal vs leather.

Perhaps if the engineers at A.T. Cross had spent some time getting trained at Coach Leatherware, they would have learned that you cannot inspect leather merchandise the way you inspect metal products. One is a natural material, the other is industrial. So for all the time I spent at Mark Cross, we scratched our heads in trying to figure out how to explain to the engineers that these handbags, or belts, or wallets were not damaged, and that real leather has numerous surface variations. All the products were made in Italy, in the same factory that made Gucci and other luxury brands. Despite all the conflicts with the corporate office about leather vs metal, it was still one of the most fun jobs I had. This was mainly because of my boss, Edward Wasserberger. Edward was in charge of product development so I worked mostly with him and traveled to Italy with him several times a year.

There is no better way to describe Edward than to compare him to Inspector Clouseau from the Pink Panther movies. There was not one trip where we didn't have to deal with some hysterical accident, none of them too serious except for the time when he was sitting around his pool deck in a bathrobe and set himself on fire because in lighting a cigarette he didn't realize that he also lit the end of his bathrobe's belt. In dumping the bathrobe on the deck and jumping into the pool, the fire spread and long story short, the day was saved by the firemen from the Westhampton Fire Department. It was during my time at Mark Cross, as we used to recount our adventures in the office that we thought we should write a book about some of Edward's "accidents". Here are a few of the less dangerous adventures:

One day, in the office in New York, he came into my office with his calculator in hand telling me that for some reason his phone wasn't working and could he use my phone. I asked him what exactly was wrong with his phone. He showed me the calculator and said "Here, you can see for yourself", giving me the calculator. I told him, "This is not a phone, Edward, it's a calculator". "Oh" he said, and went back to his office.

In all fairness, his phone, just like all the office phones was one of those multi line phones which I can see could be confused with a calculator, same size, had numbers on it … oh yeah! Very easy to confuse.

During all our trips to Italy, we traveled separately - it was something about security and the danger of unexpected catastrophes, like a plane crash. So I used to fly into Milan and he flew to Switzerland where he had meetings with some European associates. We would then meet in Varese where our main factory was located.

Invariably, every time we met downstairs at the hotel the next day for breakfast, Edward appeared with a bandage on his nose. The first time, I asked him, "What happened to you?" His answer: "Those damn Swiss banks. The glass doors are so clean, you can't tell it's a glass door so I walked into it and hit my nose". Needless to say, after that explanation, on subsequent trips I didn't ask any more about the bandage on the nose, I would just remark, "Those damn clean Swiss, huh?" He just shrugged.

One day, while walking in Florence on a very narrow sidewalk across the street from the Uffizi Gallery, Edward, our Italian representative, Giovanna and I had to walk single file because there was just no room on the sidewalk for even 2 people to walk next to each other. Giovanna was in the front, me behind her and Edward behind me. As we were all talking, Giovanna asked Edward something and after hearing no answer she stopped and turned around. So did I. Edward was nowhere to be seen. So we walked back several steps around a bend and there he was: he fell into a hole in the sidewalk, his shoe got caught in something and he was struggling to get his foot out. No injuries, but we decided that from then on, he would walk in front us.

As we were walking back to our hotel one late afternoon, we passed a small store where he decided to stop and buy some socks. The store looked closed because we could see the owner, a woman, alone and apparently taking some inventory from this very tall box right behind her. Each time she took out some item, she placed it on the counter and wrote something in a book on the counter. The store was very narrow, barely 12 feet wide, what with the display cases, the counter and space behind, there was barely room for more than about 5 people, if they all lined up next to each other in front of the counter. Edward assumed the store was open so he just walked in with us behind him. He was about 5 feet away from the woman who didn't notice us but got so startled when he said "Buona Sera, signora" that she stepped back and …. fell into the box with her arms and feet in the air – like a cockroach. We all rushed over to help her out of the box. He bought his socks and we kept an eye on the woman to make sure she was not having a heart attack. We could barely walk after this, from the pain of laughing.

One day, while in Varese at the factory which was in a quite gorgeous old church, we went to the back rooms for a meeting with the owner, Mr. Ricci. While we were all sitting in his office, Edward got up to go to the bathroom. A few minutes later, we heard a horrendous crash, ran out of the office and there was a tableau that is hard to describe. Edward was on the floor having broken through a mirrored door into a tiny office with a startled looking man at a tiny desk. It turns out that in coming out of the bathroom, which was a step higher than the floor, he tripped on the step, fell forward into what he thought was just a mirrored wall but was actually a door to a secret office – the tiny office of the secret accountant, the one with the black books. This discovery was sort of embarrassing even though we all knew that Italian companies kept 2 separate sets of books, the real ones and the ones for the tax man. But that wasn't our business, so needless to say, this accidental finding was just another one in the annals of Edward's Inspector Clouseau routines. Back in New York, the office was in stitches when they heard about it.

One final one, which is one of my favorites was a hotel misadventure. In Florence, where we also had some factories, we used to stay at the Lungarno Hotel, on the Borgo San Jacopo. Edward was very well known there since he stayed at that hotel all the time, long before I came on board. One day, just before we were supposed to meet downstairs to go to one of our factories, he called my room with a little panicked voice. What was the problem? He had no pants!

I didn't understand what that meant until he explained that when he gave some clothes to the hotel cleaners, while he was still in his bathrobe, he didn't realize that he gave them ALL his pants therefore he had none to wear. I had to call the front desk to tell them to call the laundry company and ask them to send back the laundry truck so Edward could get back a pair of pants. Of course we were 2 hours late to the meeting but at least the Lungarno hotel staff had something to talk about for a couple of days.

Apparently, this was not the first time this had happened. When I used to recount all these stories to his brother George, who was the general manager and his niece Leah, who was in charge of the catalogue, they basically just shook their heads, as in "So, what else is new?" I suppose there were a lot more stories than the ones I experienced.

The only unpleasant experience I had was in Como, when both my American & French passports were stolen from my handbag. Aside from the inconvenience, at that time there were also savage attacks by a group called The Red Brigade, a left wing terrorist group and our fear was that the passports would end up in their hands and be used for illegal travel.

Figure 18 - With Giovanna and Edward in Como, 1985

The replacement for the French passport I was able to get right away from the French consulate because they called several hotels in which I stayed previously and they got the required information right away.

The American passport was a bit of a problem because I definitely didn't sound American at the consulate, and I had no way of proving that I was a citizen or that I even had an American passport, because all these hotels had my French passport information. The reason was precisely because I was afraid of these Red Brigade groups that targeted US citizens.

I had to call my husband in New York and have him try to find my citizenship papers and fax them to the consulate. While we were waiting for this information, I remembered a hotel where I stayed the previous year and hoped that maybe there I registered with the US passport. I was right; I stayed at the Villa San Michele which was once a monastery and it was also where Napoleon stayed when he was in Florence. Yes, I have a thing about Napoleon. And fortunately, they had my US passport information, probably because in previous years there were not as many threats to US citizens.

But being paranoid as I am about my identity, I still had these visions that my passports were being used for some nefarious purpose and that my name was on some suspect list and that I would be met by the FBI upon my return to NY. Luckily, I was completely ignored at passport control at Kennedy Airport.

Hermès

In 1987 I was recruited for a job at the Hermès corporate office in New York. This took several months to negotiate simply because I really didn't want to leave my job at Mark Cross.

The job was to be the assistant to the Vice President of Merchandising and Marketing so that I could learn the ropes and then take over her job in a couple of years as she was planning to retire. It sounded nice but I really didn't want a promotion – as I said earlier, I never had any career ambitions and I never liked being in charge of other people. It had nothing to do with money – I never cared about that. I just didn't have the killer instinct; I guess because I did not grow up in a free society so it was just not part of my persona.

But after many of my friends told me I was nuts not to take the job, I finally conceded; however, it turned out to be only after a tragic accident which again made me hesitant since I'm highly superstitious. The manager in question was the victim of a deadly road accident, so now I actually had to take over her job and not train for it. I was terrified but the CEO of the American division of the company was very encouraging and supportive so I accepted. The CEO was Chrys Fisher and I learned much from him as he was not only very intelligent, but came from a very solid retail background that started with a family business of very high end stores, followed by Neiman Marcus, before he came to Hermès. One thing that stayed with me to this day was an expression he had that even my husband Shelly adopted and uses whenever appropriate; it refers to setting up rules so that "How ya starts is how ya finish". Oh yes, he was from Oklahoma.

But before I could actually come on board, I had to be vetted by the Chairman in Paris, Jean-Louis Dumas. So I was sent to Paris and met with Mr. Dumas who was not only incredibly charming but also a very talented artist, which I was not aware of and as we were chatting he drew some cartoons for me based on stories I told him about my background. They were very clever and amusing drawings including one of a cat because I told him I had a cat.

Figure 19 - Drawings by Jean Louis Dumas during interview at Hermes, Paris, March, 1988

I learned that he also drew all the illustrations on the Hermès ads. Truly, he was a very impressive man.

One aspect of my background that seemed a perfect fit for Hermès was that I was coming from an American company with the same background as Hermès. Mark Cross, was also a family business like Hermès. Both companies were started in 1845 and both started out making leather saddles for the upper class. Then, with the passing years, as society moved from the horse and buggy era to the automobile era, both companies began to expand their manufacturing to other leather products, such as handbags, belts, etc. The two really had a strikingly similar history.

Figure 20 - dinner party in Paris 1989 with Jean Louis Dumas and Chrys Fisher

My time at Hermès was interesting and fun but also involved a lot of travel: to Paris for the seasonal buys and to the company stores all around the country. At some point I think I lost it when I got off a plane and didn't know where I was. I gave the taxi driver the name of the hotel and he told me there was no such hotel in Dallas. I said "Dallas? We're in Dallas?"

At this point the driver stopped the taxi, looked back at me and said "Where do you think you are?" Now I began to panic because I realized that I had completely lost it and sheepishly said, "So this is not Chicago"? The driver must have cursed under his breath but was very polite and said, "No Miss, this is not Chicago, it's Dallas." OK, the thing is I was going to Chicago the following week so I must have been thinking about that, or I had too many Bloody Marys on the flight.

After I admitted that I was a bit confused, he asked me again that now that I know where I was, did I know the name of the hotel where I was staying in Dallas. Again, I completely blanked out. All I could tell him was that it was a very pretty pink building. He sat there thinking and mentioned a few hotels none of which sounded familiar until he said, "The Mansion?" I yelled "Yes, yes, the Mansion". Unfortunately, that was not the end of it.

Now that I arrived at the hotel where they knew me well from past visits, I was taken to my room and about a half hour later I came down to the lobby to get a taxi to go to the Hermès store. The receptionist called a taxi and asked me where I would like to go. The problem was I forgot the store address! So now I was thinking how to get out of this one without looking like a complete idiot so I said, "Oh, I'm just going to the Hermès store" hoping she knew the address. Luckily she did – I guess everybody knew that address, Highland Park Village, since it was a very upscale outdoor mall. Whew!

I don't know what happened to me that day – I was really afraid that I was losing my mind. Fortunately, I at least remembered the manager's name. After this visit, all went back to normal and I got back to New York, not Cleveland.

The Bedford Impersonation

This is just an anecdote about speaking French in a muffled tone and the influence of aristocracy. During all our trips to Paris for the seasonal merchandise buys, we all stayed at the Bedford Hotel because it was close to the Hermès store and not too expensive. Well, at least not at that time, in the late 80s-early 90s. However, the more stores we opened around the US, the more people there were in our group since all the store managers had to be there plus about 8-10 people from the corporate office, and going out to dinner as a group was a challenge.

Some of the people from our corporate office and one or two store managers spoke French so they could go wherever they wanted on their own. I felt responsible to babysit the store managers who either did not speak French, or this was their first time in Paris so I always led a group of about 10-12 people.

To make a reservation for 12 people in a Paris restaurant is not an easy task. A couple of times it worked when I said we were calling from Hermès so they accommodated us. But after a while, that didn't work so I tried something else.

I said in a very fast and I guess somewhat muffled voice, *"Bonjour, Je vous appele du Bedford et nous aimerions une réservation pour 10 personnes vers 8 heures*." Meaning, "I'm calling from the Bedford for a reservation for 10 people at 8 o'clock ". They confirmed immediately. Why? The person on the other end thought I was saying that that I was calling for the Duke of Bedford so the gates were wide open! The pronunciation in French of "du Bedford" (from the Bedford) sounded like *Duc de Bedford*! Frankly, I didn't even know if there was such a person as the Duke of Bedford, but who cares? It worked every time.

After a while, not seeing a Duke of Bedford within our group, they wised up to the scam and figured out that we were calling from the hotel named Bedford so no more reservations for 12 people. Oh well, it was good while it lasted.

Because I traveled around the country so much during my time at Hermès, I also learned some interesting characteristics about local social structures in various parts of the country. My travels to store openings and evaluations of local stores who wanted to carry Hermès products took me to almost every state in the union except for Alaska, South Dakota and New Mexico.

One of the more interesting states to me was Texas. Although our products were sold in several high end stores in various cities in the state, we only opened two company owned stores, in Dallas and Houston. And that's the interesting part – the difference between the elite customer base in Dallas and the one in Houston.

Though I noticed some differences during the opening parties in terms of the fashion trends, the real difference became apparent months later when we analyzed the sales. The store in Houston was doing much better than the store in Dallas. I was curious why so I spoke at length with the two store managers and they explained it quite clearly. The Dallas society ladies did not shop locally – they flew, in their private planes of course, to Beverly Hills, New York or straight to Paris for their shopping expeditions. The Houston ladies, though just as wealthy as the Dallas ones, were much more down to earth and completely unpretentious so they did shop in Houston stores.

It was an interesting differentiation which clarified the sales statistics. By the way, Hermes, had to make special ties for several Texas stores such as Malouf's because the men were so tall, the ties had to be made longer. I loved that! Those tall Texas guys!

THE 1989 SAN FRANCISCO EARTHQUAKE

Aside from various frightening experiences which I usually attributed either to bad luck or a nefarious conspiracy by a nasty government, there was also this innate Jewish guilt which always surfaced whenever I felt that I had a role in the cause of some catastrophe. That's what happened in October 1989 when I flew to San Francisco to attend a party for Vogue at the San Francisco Hermès store.

They needed someone from the corporate office and everybody else had other engagements so I was the unlucky winner. Just as an aside, one thing I never felt comfortable with was cocktail parties. And considering all the store openings we did around the country, special events, and other celebrations and launches, as a Vice President of the company I was a permanent fixture at all these events which ultimately became just a blur of people, champagne and hors d'oeuvres.

The thing was, and still is, that I'm not good at small talk in a room full of people I don't know. I'm great on flirting one on one, mostly with older men, but cocktail party chatter was something I never managed to master.

Figure 21 - *Chatting with Stanley Marcus*

Here I am trying to flirt with Stanley Marcus, of Neiman Marcus fame at some store opening, probably in Houston, 1990.

As I was getting ready for the party at around 5PM in my hotel room, while I was in the bathroom putting on make-up, I suddenly felt dizzy which I found strange since I know that I tend to get dizzy when I drink alcohol, and I did have a glass of wine at lunch but now, 4 hours later I'm feeling drunk?

I realized that something was not right when the wall tiles in the bathroom started falling into the bathtub, the TV in the closet at the foot of the bed fell on the bed, and through the window I could see the TransAmerica needle tower waving back and forth. I ran out in the hall in my underwear just as the chandelier came crashing down, luckily about 5 feet away from my door. That's when I saw hotel staff running down the steps and yelling "Get out, it's an earthquake".

I ran back into my room and took a dress that was on the bed and 3 shoes and ran down the steps from the 10th floor of the Four Season Hotel along with other guests to the lobby. The lobby was full of people in various states of undress all walking around like zombies.

I got dressed in a hurry and gave the extra shoe to the concierge to hold for me. Since the store was only a few blocks away, on Union Square, I walked over to make sure everybody was OK. On the way there, the street was full of broken glass from shattered windows in various buildings. I walked in the middle of the street because I was afraid of getting hit by falling debris which kept coming down. When I got to the store, I was happy to see everybody was OK only our party dishes were all smashed. Needless to say, there was no party since the entire city was shut down – no electricity, no phones, nothing was working. Except for two elegant ladies who showed up as if nothing had happened. I guess they were such devoted party goers that no 6.9 earthquake was going to get in their way.

The lucky thing was that the manager of the building had a cell phone – one of those phones the size of a shoe – and he let us all use it to call our families and tell them that we were OK. Now, we all stared at each other not knowing what to do. The Hermès store manager, Cheri Threadgill, one of the coolest women I ever met, suggested that we simply close the store since there was no business going to be done that day and we were afraid of potential looting since the square was full of people, all having run out of the various buildings in the area for fear of being crushed.

I agreed and we decided to drive by her house to see what condition her building was in. The trip was really scary, there were so many scrambled buildings and in the distance we could see huge fires in the Marina area.

Her house was still standing but there was a huge diagonal crack across the front of the building. She didn't want to go in and so she asked me what I wanted to do. I said "I want to get the f... out of here". So we decided to go back to my hotel and collect my luggage. We walked up 10 flights with a flash light; no candles were allowed in case there were gas leaks. We got my suitcase and walked down the 10 flights again. At this point, there was no way to get to the airport because there was not a car or taxi on the road. So we decided that she would go home and see what the status of her apartment was and I would just hang around the hotel until I could find some way of getting out. Outside the hotel and down the street and the Square, it was wall to wall people - still looking shell shocked. Nobody knew what to do and many of the hotel guests at the Four Seasons had come to San Francisco for the World Series game at Candlestick Park.

The city was packed. So there I stood with everybody else, just staring at the street where nothing was happening. Then, all of a sudden, I saw a black limo coming down the street and slowing down in front of the hotel. I ran over to the car and asked the driver if he was picking up somebody. He said, "Yes, you!" I said "Really?" and he said, "Really, where do you want to go?" I screamed, "ANYWHERE – just get me out of here, to any airport". I got my luggage and hopped into the car thinking that God or some angel was watching over me. I never felt such relief. This was a real limo with a bar and a TV. I turned on the TV and that was the first time I saw what actually happened and again I thought that someone was watching over me because the highway that was most seriously hit and which had several fatal accidents was the highway I had been on only 2 hours before the earthquake, on my way back from Costa Mesa.

The road we were on was not intact either – there were deep fissures several feet long that were something straight out of some apocalyptic movie. After the third such fissure the driver deftly avoided, I fell asleep and didn't wake up until the driver woke me up and said that we were at a hotel near the airport that would take me in at no cost in a makeshift common area laid out with emergency beds for other stranded people. He also told me that there was a flight in the morning to NY via Los Angeles and that the hotel shuttle would take us there at no cost.

I thanked him profusely not only for driving me here but for arranging the whole stay. I paid him $125 in cash – I only had $150 and he said that I should keep the rest so that I could buy some food at the airport. I wish I had taken his information so that I could have thanked him again once I got home but I was so disoriented at the time that I never thought of it. I had never stayed in a shelter before so this was a new thing for me. What they did is to remove all the tables and chairs from the dining room and replaced them with beds, sheets, pillows and covers. There was also a long table laid out with snacks, cookies and drinks. It was the nicest thing in the world. This was the Red Roof Inn and I did send them a very warm thank you letter when I got home. During the flight home, I was a nervous wreck. Every time I heard an engine roar, I thought it was an earthquake. You can't forget that sound, it penetrates your body.

The next day at the office, everybody greeted me with crossed fingers as though they were trying to ward off evil spirits. Though nobody at Hermès knew me in the 70s, they did hear about some of my travel misadventures before the San Francisco disaster, like the Newfoundland landing, which was the reason for the crossed fingers – it just seemed like I attracted bad luck when traveling. After that, every time we had to take a trip, my colleagues would first check with my assistant Gloria to find out what flight I was on so that they could book other flights. But then Gloria would always come in to my office and rat them out to me. I found it highly amusing and being the superstitious freak that I was, I certainly understood their apprehension. This didn't stop me from torturing them afterwards – during some fun dinner in Paris.

Now, what does this have to do with Jewish guilt? Well, I was sure God punished me for flying to San Francisco for such a frivolous thing as a party! Of course the fact that earthquakes are common in California and it was my bad luck to be there at the wrong time was irrelevant. I was convinced it my fault. When I told this to my psychiatrist, he just looked at me, so I asked him if he thought I was crazy. He responded "Certifiable". Well, it's always good to know where you stand.

We don't want to end up on a sad note, so here is something more upbeat. Every year we opened a new store in some city in the US or Canada, a large group from the office would travel to that location in order to set up the merchandise, the books, the computers and other details incidental to the opening of a new retail store.

There were also opening night parties in all those locations where the crème de la crème of that city would be invited to the opening. For example, in Washington DC, we got to visit the White House, had receptions at the French embassy and other social events or visits to important landmarks in the area. I think one of my favorites was in Boston, where one of the receptions was in the house of a descendant of John Adams. How much more historic can you get?

My silliest escapade was at the opening in Houston. After the big party with oil barons, our plans included a tour of NASA headquarters where we were given a detailed tour by an astronaut and took ridiculous pictures as space cadets. But then who wouldn't want to take a picture flying around in a space suit?

Figure 22 - Space cadet

The following day we went horseback riding on the beach in Galveston. Needless to say, we were all expert riders since we were experts in selling the most luxurious saddles, right? Yeah, sure. All expert riders, except me, the Vice President of Merchandising.

My horse turned out to be a schizoid lunatic even though I asked the guide if he could give her some Valium because she looked nervous to me even before I mounted her. And I was right – turned out that my horse, Daisy, didn't like the guide's horse, and whenever he came near me, she would take off regardless of how I reined her in. So this beast was galloping ahead of everybody and my team was in stitches while they casually trotted in the sand, all together, like a posse.

Then, to add insult to injury, my Daisy decided that she needed to take a leak, in the water. So all of a sudden, she just walked into the water and did her business and I couldn't do a thing about it. Everybody was laughing their heads off – I was mortified. When we got back to the stables, I told the guide that he was lucky there were so many people around, otherwise I would have done something very bad to him. He was amused and why not? He could tell all his friends about the city slicker from New York who got trashed by his horse.

One of the most pleasant things about my time at Hermes is the fact that all our business trips included the entire team. Visiting our factories, whether they made scarves, leather goods, accessories, fragrances or other products, gave us a valuable learning experience as to how Hermes products were created and made.

Figure 23- The US team at the Vaudreuil fragrance factory

Figure 24 - The scarf factory in Lyon

Considering today's frenzy about Hermès I suspect many readers are curious whether or not I personally had a lot of their products. The answer is of course, yes. But many of them, like scarves, were samples that we used to give to the employees at the end of the season. And though we all had generous employee discounts, none of us were rabid consumers as the market seems to be filled with now. In fact, at one point I remember I exchanged a large handbag – one of the first Birkin bags - for 2 large wool and cashmere throws because they were useful in cold weather while the bag was clumsy and heavy.

Most of us loved the Kelly bag because it was very practical since in addition to the short handle, which is the way Princess Grace (Kelly) used to carry it, it had a detachable shoulder strap. That's very convenient if you're not just a "lunch lady" who gets out of her limo into a restaurant. Sometimes you need your hands free for other activities, so a shoulder bag is much more convenient. Since many of us had the same bag, usually the same color, the factory got us gold initials to be affixed to the flap so we that we didn't walk away with each other's bags which happened all the time especially in Paris at meetings. A side note: most of the handbags as well as many other products were named after a specific person – a family member, a good customer, anybody that had an impact in the design of a specific item, such as Grace Kelly, or Jane Birkin, or the Constance, one of my favorite handbags, named after an Hermes family member.

In retrospect, I don't think the fashion industry was a good fit for me. The business end yes, the fashion, no. I was never a fashionista, I had and still have the taste of some hillbilly European widow – Black. Though I still have some faded Pink Chanel outfits – my outrageous color departure from the morbid Black uniform, my style was always very classic, or boring, to be honest.

The reason I liked mostly the business aspect of all these jobs is because I most enjoyed analyzing the statistics; it's always about numbers. The most exciting application in retail is the Open-to-Buy, my favorite analytical and predictive tool. I really should have been an actuary. Alas, at the time I didn't even know this profession existed.

Frankly Fake Finishes

After taking a leave of absence from Hermès to take care of my father who was in and out of hospice care, I pondered what I really wanted to do. I knew I didn't want to be in the fashion industry again after having spent 25 years there. Also, after Hermès, everything else paled in comparison.

I felt that it was time to do something else, but what?

Since I never had any career or life ambitions, visions, desires, interests or plans, I always thought it was a character flaw especially in a free and competitive society like the US. After all, part of the American dream was that you could be anything you wanted. There was no such thing where I grew up which always makes me wonder what would have happened if we had stayed in Romania. There is no question I would not have been able to go to college unless I moved to another city and changed my name. The only reason my cousin in Bucharest was accepted to the university to study engineering was because nobody knew she was Jewish. The family changed its name from Ebenstein to a typical Romanian name, ending in a vowel.

Obviously, I did not grow up in an environment where plans were made for higher education. Certainly not after my math prize was degraded, and I was thrown out of school because some Communist thug wanted my father's job.

So after Hermès I started indulging in a passion I pursued while working at Mark Cross, namely trompe l'oeil painting. I did occasionally indulge in painting, both oil and acrylics over the years.

But during buying trips to Italy, I started taking courses in trompe l'oeil painting in Florence and then at The Finishing School in Great Neck. I really became passionate about it and started practicing in the apartment by painting rooms and specific walls in a variety of styles. All this was rather disconcerting to Shelly - when he used to come home from the office he never knew what he'd find: a stone cave, marble columns, night skies, birds flying over clouds, endless gardens, crazy wood inlays – it was a an incredible mish mash. But hey, where else could I practice to my heart's desire?. Then, the piece de resistance which generated an article in The New York Times home section, defined my career for the next 2 years which then morphed into a derivative career.

This may sound very convoluted but it's precisely the kind of trajectory many people embark on if they haven't made specific choices in college or at other times in their lives. What I did is buy a computer, a 386 PC to be exact. It was just at the beginning of Windows, actually, Windows 3.0 as well as some basic graphics software.

Since we had no room for a computer and all its accessories, I decided to buy a computer cabinet so that when not in use, it would just be another cabinet in the living room. But could I live with just another boring looking cabinet? Of course not. So I started painting it, added moldings and other decorative elements and basically transformed it into a neo-Empire looking piece of furniture. A friend of mine who was a Public Relations maven, sent a picture of

It Began in Transylvania

Figure 25 – NY Times article

the cabinet to the New York Times, and after the picture appeared in the paper, I was deluged with phone calls from people who wanted a variety of trompe l'oeil projects – walls, ceilings, floors, furniture.

After looking at some of those projects I realized I did not want to be some Vatican painter and hang out on a platform under ceilings. I took on just one project, a derivative sun design sent to me by the interior designer of the client. It was to be painted as wood inlays on the floor of her Park Avenue apartment.

The project turned out to be very nice and the client was very nice. One day, I also got to meet Robert Redford in the elevator. He apparently lived in the same building. What more could one ask for from a paint job than to meet Robert Redford in an elevator? Right?

The next project was a round table in the foyer of a house in Southampton. This is the one that really turned me off from hanging out in other people's homes. It was in the middle of the winter and the owners of the house wanted me to work during the week while they were in their city apartment which was perfectly normal.

Figure 26 - Sun design in a Park Avenue apartment

However, they turned off the heat and water so that I was freezing while painting and if I had to use the bathroom, I had to go to a restaurant in town. And these were friends of ours, not just clients.

So ended my career as a Michelangelo wannabe.

But, the painting bug still bugged me and with my 25 years in the wholesale/retail business, the two suddenly converged and I came up with a more suitable strategy: I decided that I would make faux painted furniture and accessories which could be done much faster than the Sistine Chapel and which could be sold at retail. In other words, I was going to be a manufacturer and vendor! Since I knew every aspect of this business, it was not a difficult strategy to implement. All I needed was the product.

Well, it's one thing to paint a wall or a large piece of furniture which in itself takes an enormous amount of time. It's a different thing to paint many pieces of a single article based on orders from stores. My first orders came from stores that I had a previous relationship with while I was at Hermès, so the first one was Bergdorf Goodman.

They liked my samples of wood inlays on sets of 4 folding tables, and I got an order for 200 tables for their Christmas catalogue. Panic! How do I paint 200 tables in 2 months? And all of them identical? No way could I do this by myself and by hand.

But Eureka! My trusted 386 (soon followed by a 486) PC became the layout source to create the pattern on transparent paper, which was then cut out as a template and then applied to the surface of the tables.

But an even more perplexing question was where was I going to paint 200 tables? Certainly not in my 1 bedroom apartment in the city. Ah, but I had a large basement in the house in East Hampton. So the basement became a paint studio. The amount of paints, solvents, brushes and other tools generated daily trips to the Village Hardware store in East Hampton where the staff probably thought I was nuts. I was there almost every day buying supplies. The other store that I hounded almost daily was the Golden Eagle since I was always looking for specific oil pigments like Cadmium Yellow; I mean it couldn't have been just Yellow, it had to be Cadmium Yellow!

The first shipment went ok. After a few more orders from other stores, we started to have some problems which were often quite comical but certainly not very professional.

I say we, because I had an assistant, Aline, whom I knew from Hermes as her mother was a great scarf designer at the company. Aline was very talented in painting the tables, but between the two of us, we were not that great at packing and shipping. The issue was that the shipping boxes were very large as they had to contain 4 folding tables and a rack. So we sometimes had a few accidents. Like the time we got a call from the Jacobson store in Jackson, Michigan that one of the boxes contained 2 crickets. Another time, we got a call from some other store that they found a tuna fish sandwich in one of the boxes. That kind of cleared up where my lunch disappeared the week before. I guess I shipped my lunch in one of the boxes. We couldn't do anything about the crickets, they were everywhere.

After about 6 months of working out of the basement, Shelly got really annoyed because the whole house smelled like paint and chemical spirits and the basement was a paint stained disaster.

So we decided to move the "studio" to the city, and found space in the Chelsea area. But I no longer had Aline so I had to figure out how I was going to paint hundreds of tables and other products myself, by hand.

I didn't have to look too hard for an assistant. The guy who delivered my sandwiches from the restaurant next door became my assistant in his off hours and the rest of my family became the packing and shipping department.

I taught Louis, the delivery guy, how to paint the wood grains on the paper cutouts and he was great. He did about 20 tables a day. My husband, the attorney, was the shipping clerk since he told me he once worked at A&S (anyone remember that store?) packing lamps when he was in college. My 3-year old nephew Paul was hired to place stamps on the envelopes with invoices and my mother brought food for everybody.

All of this took place in a studio in Chelsea. The products were a great success and the buyer from Bergdorf always called me whenever some celebrity bought the table set. I cannot mention anybody but I remember being a bit envious when I was told of one well known customer who bought my painted objects while I didn't have even one of her father's paintings. I leave it to your imagination to figure out who she was.

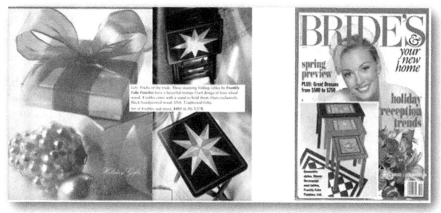

Figure 27 - Bergdorf Goodman Christmas 1991 Catalogue and Bride's Magazine 1992

The following year I did a collection of playing cards that looked as though they fell on a table – of course it was a Royal Flush. Remember, I was a poker freak in my younger days.

Figure 28 - Bergdorf Goodman Christmas 1993 Catalogue

One project which unfortunately fell through due to a variety of logistical problems was an order from Neiman Marcus for a set of His and Hers pianos for one of their Christmas catalogs which always featured some outrageous product, like his and hers planes and other out of the world offerings. The His piano was to be painted in a variety of marquetry wood grains, the Hers was to be painted with encrusted jewels.

Oh well, it was disappointing but in one sense I was relieved because it seemed like a very ambitious project to complete in a very short period of time.

There are three things that ultimately made me give up this business:

The more merchandise I sold, the more money I lost. One of the problems was charge backs – I believe this is a buried revenue stream for large stores. One shipment of 20 boxes, had a spelling error on the accompanying invoices which when scanned by the store's receiving department's computers, generated a charge back of $150 for each invoice. Since my margin was not that big in the first place, having a staff payroll (my 3-year nephew was paid $0.25 per stamp) and other expenses, this kind of spelling error penalty contributed to putting me out of business – at least with big stores.

Another factor was one of my neighbors. It was some sort of boxing studio and they kept kicking the wall between us causing all my objects on the wall shelves to keep falling off. Nothing broke since they were all wooden objects but it was very annoying to walk into the studio in the morning and find all my plates, vases, boxes, frames, etc., on the floor.

Figure 29 – Some items from the Frankly Fake Finishes collection.

Finally, I constantly smelled of paint, and the paint solvents made me nauseated. I decided that the only way for me to continue in this business was to have the stuff manufactured elsewhere and have it drop shipped. But that meant I would have had to find a factory in Italy or China which was not part of my original love affair with trompe l'oeil painting.

So I decided to quit while I was still ahead and stick to computers which were very clean, didn't give me a headache and didn't stink. The only thing I missed? Here we go again. There was this little rodent which came around every day at 4:30PM and nibbled on my feet. I used to give him crackers and we played cat and mouse. I would pick him up and he would wriggle out of my hand. I can't forget his timely appearances – I really should have investigated why he appeared every day at exactly 4:30PM. How was that possible? I didn't see him wearing a watch or maybe he was a she? I don't know, I forgot to look under the tail. That was the only thing I missed after I moved out of that studio - my little Micro mouse (named after Microsoft).

Technology phase

After the Frankly Fake Finishes business folded, I was a little lost – somehow I no longer had that fire in the belly for work, any kind of work. Maybe it was because of the crisis in my family when I ended up being responsible for taking care of my father who was very ill and was given just months to live.

Maybe I was just bored with fashion which had not been my intended career choice in the first place, but the reality was that I simply never even thought about the concept of work. All the jobs in the fashion industry were serendipitous – I noticed that I never lasted more than 4-5 years anywhere.

It seemed like every time I got excited about a job because I would be responsible for carving out some new path, process or strategy, etc., I was very dedicated and involved. But by the time the project was finished and all it then required was maintenance, I started getting bored. Maybe I should have always looked for short term consulting jobs – seemed like I always needed new challenges.

In any event, while I was in-between jobs, I began to get involved in emerging technologies with personal computers. This was sometime before the web had appeared. Maybe it was also a good escape from the depression and sadness of taking care of my father who was in and out of hospice care.

As mentioned before, my first PC was a 386 - a step ahead of the 8088 which I believe was the original PC dinosaur, black screen, white text. The 386 cost $5,000 which seems inconceivable today but there it was. It was also the first PC to run Windows, therefore it was in color and also had a CD-ROM drive in addition to the 3 other drives: the C hard drive and the A and B floppy drives for 5 ½ and 3 ½ inch floppy disks. Oh yes – it was really state of the art! Having already had some experience from the unfortunate computer programming classes 20 years earlier in France, I did have a basic understanding of this new operating system called DOS which seemed a lot simpler than the era of punch cards. In case anyone is interested, DOS is the abbreviation for Disc Operating System

I literally buried myself in computer manuals and learned everything on my own by following every exercise in the manuals for DOS, WordPerfect 5.1, DrawPerfect and CorelDraw 1.1 on my fancy new PC. I did have some help from a few IT people who were employed by companies where I had worked before, and they set up the machine and installed the programs I wanted.

By 1993, I became really good at it to the point that I was able to set up a BBS (Bulletin Board Service) which was the precursor for today's web and email. Many of these BBS systems were free while others charged a fee to access their information. The process involved dialing in via a modem to the BBS's server which was nothing more than a PC with several phone lines so that if a server only had 5 lines, then only 5 people could dial in at the same time. Everybody else would get a busy signal. However, once you were connected, you could search for any information that was available on that computer. By the way, the speed of the modems at that time was something like [19 bps] which was about as fast as downloading a movie today on your cellphone when you're in an area that has a one-bar tower signal.

The search methods were also primitive as well as comical. Instead of the typical search engines used today on the web, BBSs could be searched only via Telnet (don't even ask what that is) with search tools named Archie,

Gopher or Veronica, depending on what you were searching for. Who said geeks don't have a sense of humor? Actually, most of the geeks I met during my career were the most fun and witty people.

Not having grown up in the US, I didn't realize these were comic book characters but ultimately it didn't matter. I was able to find whatever information I needed, like a picture of a Trojan horse which I needed for a presentation I was doing at a bank as part of one of my consulting jobs. I found the picture on the Berkeley University server by using Gopher.

In researching the various BBS software applications available from a magazine named *Boardwatch,* I learned a lot about the available options, who was using it and how. I set up a free access BBS for East Hampton with one telephone line which provided information about restaurants and hotels. That was my first foray into online technology and used it mainly to figure out how things worked. I think I had 5 subscribers.

I also attended several of the *Boardwatch* magazine conferences and the best one I remember was in California. This is where I learned what drives the online world and where the money is. Though I met many BBS operators of various systems offering a variety of services, one couple I met, a husband and wife team from some remote area in Northern California was the most hilarious. He had long hair, a long beard and no teeth. She was just barely under obese. Together they operated a BBS with 100 telephone lines, from something like a barn in the middle of nowhere. To connect to their BBS, they charged a $5.00 monthly fee. So what was their revenue? About $2,000,000 a year!

What on earth were these people selling to make so much money? Well, well, well – what else but sex, in the form of pirated photos from porno magazines which they scanned and then made available for download! That was some eye-opener. Other respectable revenues for BBSs were those that offered gambling. All of these people operated from a garage or somebody's basement and all of these were one-man businesses. Of course, not much has changed since 1993 – the three most popular subjects on the web are still sex, gambling and … go figure this one - cats!

At one of these conferences, I also I met some Microsoft people including Bill Gates who was a bit strange – he seemed to always be in another world. I saw him once walking down the hall of the hotel we were staying at, running his hand along the wall as he walked mumbling to himself. I guess that's how geniuses operate – they talk to themselves because they're their best audience? I don't know but I will always be grateful for the existence of Microsoft because of the impact it has had on my professional life ever since.

Fashion Group International

After one of those conferences, I decided that it was time to set up a BBS that was more productive than my East Hampton toy, something that would be of benefit to more people.

At that time I was also working part time at Fashion Group International, an organization of about 4,000 fashion executives around the world. It was also a time when many apparel businesses had folded and there were many unemployed fashion industry people looking for jobs. So I had this idea of setting up a BBS with a few telephone lines that would make it easy for FGI members to search for a job and/or to be found by companies looking for candidates to fill job openings. In other words, this would be an employment match making service. And yes, this was way before all those job search sites like Monster. Our BBS was established in 1993, Monster was established in 1994! So there!

What gave me the idea for this was that FGI used to send out monthly newsletters to its members which contained, among other fashion related information, job openings at various companies in the industry. As one can imagine, by the time the newsletter arrived, by mail, the jobs listed were already gone.

The fact was that FGI was a good source of employment opportunities as company executives would often inquire by phone if the organization was able to recommend someone from their membership for a job as Designer, Marketing Director, Sales Person, etc. So having the members' resumes available online in a database searchable by companies, and for companies to post job openings seemed like a good idea - a 2-way communication system. The venture would generate revenue for FGI by charging the companies a monthly fee.

Members' access was of course free. I suggested the project to the FGI Director, Margaret Hayes who presented it to the board of directors and the project was approved. Margaret Hayes was always on top of new developments, and a real asset to the organization. But I couldn't do it alone – I was still a bit new at setting up the logistics, like the telephone lines.

Through the *Boardwatch* magazine, I became acquainted with one of the most wonderful people I met over the years – a fireman named Jim Tancredi who was the Sysop (System Operator) of the BBS system he installed at the New York City Fire Department headquarters. I asked Jim whether he could help me set up this BBS and explained to him the structure of the system.

We set up one machine with 3 telephone lines and in the next FGI newsletter, we announced the service so people who had a computer could make use of this service immediately. That was when I heard some of the most hysterical comments from members who bought a computer and would call me whenever they had some technical problem. So here it goes:

1) The cup holder is too large for my coffee mug, should I get a larger cup so it doesn't fall out?

"What cup holder? Where is it?"
"You know, on the left side of the big thing that's on the floor, there is a button and when you press it, this tray with a hole comes out"

"Diane, that's not a cup holder, it's a CD-ROM drive. Please don't push that button anymore if you don't have a disk to put in".

2) The pedal doesn't reach the floor – the cable is too short.

"What pedal?" I ask
"You know, the pedal, like on a sewing machine"
"That's not a pedal, Susan, it's a mouse, it needs to stay on the desk "

3) It says "Click for more information", but nothing happens when I click

"Where do you click, Jane?"
"I don't know, I just click"
"Well, you have to put the mouse on the word <u>Click</u>, which is underlined and the mouse arrow icon then turns into a hand icon, right?
"Oh wow, yes, thanks!

My pleasure! Can someone please get me a drink? Or a Valium?

Well, it was 1993 so I must congratulate these ladies anyway for simply having the courage to buy a computer.

But the best one had nothing to do with computers. On a previous fashion industry job, an employee who was responsible for decorating the store windows came into the office with a beautiful plant in a porcelain container. She asked my assistant to show her how to use the fax machine to fax the plant to management for approval. It took us months to get over this one.

At that time, I was using WordPerfect 5.1 for DOS as my word processor. Also at that time, tech support was free - probably because there simply weren't as many people using PCs as there have been over the years. And all beginners sometime needed help with issues that were just beyond our comprehension of this new technology. So here is a typical anecdote from that era:

Actual dialog of a former Wordperfect Customer Support employee:

"Welch Hall computer assistant; may I help you?"
"Yes, well, I'm having trouble with WordPerfect."
"What sort of trouble?"
"Well, I was just typing along, and all of a sudden the words went away.",
"Went away?"
"They disappeared."
"Hmm. So what does your screen look like now?"
"Nothing."
"Nothing?"
"It's blank; it won't accept anything when I type."
"Are you still in WordPerfect, or did you get out?"
"How do I tell?"
"Can you see the C:\ prompt on the screen?"
"What's a sea-prompt?"
"Never mind. Can you move the cursor around on the screen?"
"There isn't any cursor: I told you, it won't accept anything I type."
"Does your monitor have a power indicator?"
"What's a monitor?"
"It's the thing with the screen on it that looks like a TV. Does it have a little light that tells you when it's on?"
"I don't know."
"Well, then look on the back of the monitor and find where the power cord goes into it. Can you see that?"
"Yes, I think so."
"Great! Follow the cord to the plug, and tell me if it's plugged into the wall."

"*Yes, it is.*"
"*When you were behind the monitor, did you notice that there were two cables plugged into the back of it, not just one?*"
"*No.*"
"*Well, there are. I need you to look back there again and find the other cable.*"
"*Okay, here it is.*"
"*Follow it for me, and tell me if it's plugged securely into the back of your computer.*"
"*I can't reach.*"
"*Uh huh. Well, can you see if it is?*"
"*No.*"
"*Even if you maybe put your knee on something and lean way over?*"
"*Oh, it's not because I don't have the right angle - it's because it's dark.*"
"*Dark?*"
"*Yes-the office light is off, and the only light I have is coming in from the window.*"
"*Well, turn on the office light then.*"
"*I can't.*"
"*No? Why not?*"
"*Because there's a power outage.*"

How he responded was much kinder than that which appears below, and which has been circulating through the web for years because this person actually knew the caller who was a professor of French. So he explained sweetly and gently that computers needed power just like office lights, and if the office lights were out, then the computer was out too, and that yes, if she hadn't saved her work she had probably lost everything she'd done so far in WordPerfect.

But what he wanted to say was this:

"A power... A power outage? Aha! Okay, we've got it licked now. Do you still have the boxes and manuals and packing stuff your computer came in?"

"Well, yes, I keep them in the closet."

"Good! Go get them, and unplug your system and pack it up just like it was when you got it. Then take it back to the store you bought it from."

"Really? Is it that bad?"

"Yes, I'm afraid it is."

"Well, all right then, I suppose. What do I tell them?"

"Tell them you're too stupid to own a computer."

IBM

After about a year of running the FGI bulletin board, I became aware of this new technology called ... the World Wide Web! Mind you, not the Internet, which had been around since 1968 and was text based, but the web with its beautiful graphics interface. Thanks to Tim Berners Lee, who unfortunately was afraid of flying in airplanes so I only saw him via video while attending some of my tech conferences.

But I must mention that the first person who introduced me the existence of the web was my friend Valery Satterwhite in 1994. I learned how to code a website by looking at the source code of the White House website. I copied the code and replaced the picture of President Clinton with some other image and bingo – I figured out how it was done.

While I was investigating this new technology, like domain registrations, ISPs, HTML, SGML, and other geeky stuff, I got a call from someone named Susan Thomas who asked whether FGI would be interested in letting her company build us a website for free. Of course we jumped at the opportunity, I registered the name FGI.ORG and within 2 weeks we had a website.

Therefore, Fashion Group was among the first websites in the fashion industry – in 1995. The only other fashion related website I was aware of was by the designer Nicole Miller because the chairman of the company, Bud Konheim, was a genius!

Susan and I remained friends ever since and I actually did some other projects with her. I built several websites on my own just as a way of practicing because it was really fascinating. That's when I got an offer to join IBM as a contractor in the developing Interactive Direct Marketing division.

IBM was certainly light years ahead of any other company I had ever worked for. This was only to be expected since it was such a different industry but it also was the very definition of corporate America. And since it was an industry in constant growth, it was exciting because of the emerging technology and the brilliant people around me who were non-stop innovators. Every day was a new discovery and we were all dizzily energized trying to keep up with the innovations. Our teams were a constant work in progress and sometimes comical for people like me who came from the outside.

One example was connecting your laptop to the local printers, wirelessly of course since all the printers were in a separate room, a rather intimidating collection of machinery. Imagine my surprise when I printed several pages of some report on a printer …. in France! I just couldn't figure out why my pages weren't on the printer since I got no error messages, it said "Printing" so where were the pages? Well, I returned to my desk and tried to print again and just before I hit the Print button, I noticed that I had received an email from an IBM employee at the office in Paris. I did not know anybody at IBM in Paris so I opened the email. Well, whadda ya know? Jean told me that my report came out on their printer, at the Paris office. Ouch! I guess I wasn't the only one who screwed up things like that because after a while, we all got personal printers on our desks.

My manager at that time was Richard Merritt, an incredibly charming and brilliant man. I was most impressed when I heard that he was on the team that developed the first ATM machine in the 1970s and that he was the first person to retrieve a $20 bill from the prototype ATM.

Since we were at the beginning of the enormous marketing possibilities on the web in 1994-1995, the head of the North America Distribution created a task force with Richard Merritt and six others to develop the architecture and framework for the marketing and sales channels on the web. The area that I was working on was defining the architecture requirements for building a digital asset library. Huh? Yeah, that was my reaction too.

At the end of the study, we produced a 300 page manual with endless charts and diagrams defining every step as to how IBM was going to leverage this new marketing and sales opportunity. I must say, that half the time I attended these meetings I barely understood what they were talking about.

The word I hate most to this day is "leverage". The corporate lingo seemed like an amalgam of words jumbled together to form sentences that were basically unintelligible, but you wouldn't dare ask "Can you please say that in English" because you would then present yourself as unworthy of hobnobbing with upper management executives. So those us who were not IBM lifers (hired straight from college) had to practice how to speak in convoluted sentences so that we appeared worthy of being in such an elite corporate environment. We decided that most of these people who were doing these unintelligible presentations would probably pretend they understood any variations of this corporate speak. So we found a piece of code called the Corporate Bullshit Generator. Every time you clicked the "make bullshit" button it would come up with terms like:

strategize visionary niches; whiteboard turn-key functionalities; e-enable bleeding-edge web-readiness; leverage mission-critical action-items

The code was very simple. It contained 3 parts of speech: subjects, verbs and objects and whenever you clicked the button, it would put together a random combination of these 3 grammatical terms. Unfortunately, I never learned corporate speak but I survived anyway.

Since most of us were recruited from outside IBM for this newly created Interactive Marketing Department, and everything was evolving, it was a bit of the Wild Wild West in terms of organization, strategy and development.

The upper management was really trying to integrate all the different divisions in order to create a unified structure. The issue was that there were rogue servers under everyone's desk – one guy was running a section of the software division from under his desk, another was running part of the various global services, it was like looking for fox holes. It took a couple of years to integrate and unify these various pieces of large divisions. But I must say that all the people I worked with were brilliant – especially Tom Loretan who came from Conde Nast. He really was one of the most creative and skilled programmers I have ever worked with.

One unpleasant episode that had nothing to do with IBM but more with my intolerance of certain foods happened at an annual marketing meeting which was always held in a different city around the country. This was in Nashville at the Opryland Resort & Convention Center.

It was a beautiful place and the meetings were in the large conference center where it was not only business but also full of entertainment provided by local artists. It was really a lot of fun. During one of these sessions, I all of a sudden started feeling very strange, My heart was beating very fast and I couldn't breathe. I don't exactly remember all the symptoms but it was enough to frighten me into leaving the auditorium with my colleague Veronica Hidalgo. She walked me out to the reception area where I sat down on one of the couches and she went to the desk to ask for an ambulance. She also called my husband in New York to tell him that something was wrong and that they were taking me to the hospital.

The ambulance arrived within 5 minutes, and they started giving me oxygen while lifting me on to the stretcher. At this point, the meeting broke up and everybody started pouring out of the auditorium so that I now had some 500 spectators as I was being hauled out to the ambulance.

The EMT people felt that I was having a heart attack. I was driven to the local hospital's emergency room and placed on a bed next to a man who was all bloodied and being held at gun point by 3 policemen. Charming! I had no idea what that was about – as long as they didn't shoot me. Fortunately our beds were separated by a curtain.

After a few hours in the emergency room where I was stabilized with oxygen and some injections, I was examined by a doctor who asked me a few questions and then almost cracked up when he disclosed his diagnosis: I had an attack of acid reflux from too much southern fried food. He must have thought to himself, "these damned Yankees, they're such wussies". Too bad, because the food was delicious.

After about 2 more hours of observation I was released while the bloody guy still had the cops with guns pointing at him. Really, really weird. Since I scared the s… out of everybody in my team, they suggested I should do something fun before I went back to NY, like? Go to see the Elvis Presley house and museum in Mississippi – a couple of hours drive. Which is what we did, thus ending a scary experience on a high note because on the road we stuck only to Tutti Frutti! (Elvis Presley, 1956). I certainly was not going to eat any more fried catfish.

One other rather disturbing event that fortunately went away as soon as it appeared, was the publication of a book named *"IBM and the Holocaust : The*

Strategic Alliance between Nazi Germany and America's Most Powerful Corporation" by Edwin Black.

It described how the IBM German subsidiary used its technology to create the numbering machines that were used to ink the numbers on prisoners' arms in the camps. There was no doubt that these were totally separate companies at the time. The US was not in the war and the scandal surrounding the book ended up being a tempest in a teapot. It's very easy to be a Monday morning quarterback, especially if you hadn't even seen the game. For someone like me, who is the daughter of Holocaust survivors and working at IBM, with this book in the news, many of my friends were wondering about my opinion about this issue. The reality was that I had no opinion. I was just curious to see how IBM handled it and they did a great job.

On the other hand, and this may be merely anecdotal, I always wondered why my mother and the rest of her family did not have those numbers tattooed on their arms. Of course I couldn't ask my mother – my parents never talked about their experience. I found out years later that by 1944, the Nazis simply ran out of ink. Wow! This is another one of those simple lessons of life – you cannot fight two wars at the same time; if they had not diverted so much time, effort and resources into killing Jews, Gypsies, homosexuals and other "undesirables", they probably would have won the war and everybody in Europe would be speaking German! Jawohl, meine Herren.

I happen to like German; it is the language of Goethe, Schiller, Beethoven and Mozart and other immortal artists. Though the Germans ran out of ink, I do know what my mother's number was as well as her sisters' numbers. My mother's number was 125.11159. This comes from a document we obtained from the Holocaust Museum in Washington that got it from the German government several years ago when they started to release wartime records. The list of these women in Auschwitz and their numbers can be seen in a PDF file: http://palmerny.com/cs/AUSCHWITZ.pdf

> **No Hiding on the Web**
>
> To the Editor:
> "Frank Racial Dialogue Thrives on the Web" (front page, March 8) mentions the "almost impenetrable anonymity" or "illusion of anonymity" people enjoy when posting messages on a discussion forum, but doesn't elaborate on this misconception.
>
> Every electronic message leaves a digital footprint. Although most people may not know, or want to know, how to trace an E-mail address, government agencies or even a dedicated hacker can do so in an instant by decrypting the header information. Actually, America Online addresses are the easiest to trace, especially with a warrant; in the case of a perceived threat to national security, even anonymous remailers can have the sender's address decrypted. So blabbermouths, beware! You never know who's monitoring your cyber-pearls of wisdom. RENEE PALMER New York, March 8, 1998

Figure 30- Letter to the Editor, New York Times, 1998

During my time at IBM, I learned so much about web code, encryptions, tracing and other parsing activities, that I always felt compelled to spread the wealth by informing others of the benefits and dangers of online activities. I especially kept track of technology articles that appeared in the news that were often incorrect in terms of the information they contained. I wrote to the New York Times several times pointing out such inaccuracies.

I departed IBM when I was eligible for retirement with a pension. Since I and others like me who were hired under a different process than most employees, we were eligible for retirement much sooner than under normal circumstances.

The great thing was that when we were hired, new hires like us were also given a hiring bonus which for me generated a buying splurge at Saks Fifth Avenue in the form of a forest green mink coat! Ah, the good old days!

Haute Cuisine Cockroaches

Though this doesn't have anything to do with IBM, it happened just as I started working there. It was several weeks before my fiftieth birthday, Shelly asked what I would like to do to celebrate this momentous occasion (excluding suicide). I thought about it for a while and then finally came up with an inspirational "I don't know". Well, he said he had some ideas, and that I could pick any one of these three:

- A huge party
- A trip to Paris
- Liposuction

Now this was something to consider. Though I love parties, and I always talk about surgical enhancements, a Paris escapade tickled my fancy since I haven't been there in a while after I left Hermès. I need an infusion of Gaelic hauteur every now and then. So, off we go for a long Washington's Birthday weekend to Paris.

Having lived and worked in Paris for many years, I came to the conclusion that like the time tested theory of the house guest welcome, I can tolerate Paris for about 3 days, after which I tend to get into skirmishes with burly taxi drivers, catatonic waiters, ill-tempered shop owners and snotty saleswomen.

Much to my surprise, I must say that this weekend was programmed in heaven. I am convinced that all of Paris was on a collective Prozac prescription. Even the weather was spectacular. The hotel was superb (The Lancaster), the staff was cuddly, and as soon as we arrived in our room, Yves Montand was singing to me "Sur les Grands Boulevards".

What more could I want to put me in a gay Paree mood?

After a bucolic three days of spontaneous activities from museums to concerts to dining and shopping, the culminating evening of this little escapade took place at the one emporium of haute cuisine that I had never had an occasion to sample. This was Lucas Carton, on Place de la Madeleine, a most delectable square in Paris, with Fauchon, Caviar Kaspia, vegetable stores and Baccarat. OK, so you can't eat Baccarat, but it is nice to look at.

The reason I picked Lucas Carton is that we used to pass in front of it every day on our way from the hotel to our office at Hermès, where I was then working and which we did several times a year for the store buys. I was always fascinated by the heavy curtains so you could never see the inside of the restaurant – I don't know, it just looked very mysterious to me. Almost forbidding. By chance, our friend Dennis MacNeil, the chef of Hamptons fame who happened to have worked at Lucas Carton during his training years, offered to call the owner and make a reservation for us because it was impossible to get a reservation if you were a mere mortal. This proved to be a double edged sword, as we soon found out.

So we finally arrived on the last night of our trip at Lucas Carton, decked out in our best finery; Shelly, in his dark blue lawyerly suit and Hermès accessories, I in my vintage itchy Chanel beige tweed suit with brown velvet piping. It also had a split in the skirt seam but that was only visible when I sat down and my thighs spread out. We were seated on a nice banquette and the flurry of waiters began their shpiel with the aperitif, Monsieur Madame here, Monsieur Madame there, the works. I think there were 3-4 waiters per table. What was interesting about the layout of this dining room is that all the tables were banquettes against the wall, there were no tables in the middle of the room. That was occupied by what looked like over a dozen waiters – I presume one waiter per table.

I do have to admit that the meal was superb – we started with Kir Royales and Shelly got intoxicated by a symphony of truffles – I had a foie gras baked and wrapped in a curly cabbage leaf - it was heavenly.

As we sat there savoring every bite, luxuriating in the elegant ambiance, the sparkling crystals and silver, the elegant tableware, the pairs of uncles and nieces at nearby tables, the latter with plunging necklines and sprayed on dresses, I froze in shock at what my peripheral vision caught at the edge of the table: a large, garden variety, pride of New York cockroach. It was making a cautious advance toward my plate of rack of lamb with rosemary in a reduced beurre blanc and pommes duchesse. My first reaction was to elbow Shelly and while smiling and looking straight ahead, I whispered "take a look to the right of my plate", whereupon his eyes bugged out as only his eyes can (which makes him a good stand in Marty Feldman, if the need should ever arise).

"What are you going to do?" he whispered without moving his lips, and also staring straight ahead so as not to attract attention. I said, that I would shoo him away making sure he doesn't fly on the table to my right, occupied by a pompous prig with a Legion d'Honneur ribbon and his mistress of a certain age. How do I know it was his mistress? Elementary my dears: she kept referring to her husband's trips with a woman and was making her own plans with the pompous Legionnaire to go to Deauville in March.

Pardon my digression here, but I must share with you a time honored tradition of the French bourgeoisie. The higher up the corporate ladder a man climbs, the more mistresses he is entitled to acquire. This applies to the wife as well: if your husband is a middle management employee, you may have only one lover. But if you husband is a PDG (CEO), you may have several – including one for special occasions. The trysts usually take place between 5 and 7 PM, you know, before dinner with the family, thus the entire tradition is referred to as "*le cinq a sept*".

Back to my vermin. With class, elegance and incredible aplomb, I gently flicked the leggy intruder off the table and saw him disappear onto the floor. I whispered a hearty good-bye and urged him to go and visit the spandexed beauties across the room with their bald companions.

But that was not to be. The damn bug came back, crawling up the side of the floor-length table cloth. Something more drastic had to be done and what followed was something that belongs in a French comedy routine. I signaled a waiter who like a personal guard was not more than 2 feet away from the table, along with the other 14 or so waiters. As he approached us, I indicated to him that I would like to whisper something. He bent over, with a pleasant, *Oui madame*, and I whispered,

"Monsieur, si vous regardez à ma droite, vous verrez une petite bête qui est en train de monter sur le coin de la nappe. J'ai essayé de l'envoyer à une autre table il y 5 minutes, mais apparemment il insiste a revenir ici. Sans doute, il espère partager mon filet d'agneau aux pommes duchesse, et je le félicite pour son bon choix, mais moi, je n'ai pas envie de partager ce soir. Est-ce que vous pourrez le dissuader de continuer dans cette mission mal conçue?"

Basically translated, "Sir, there is a cockroach crawling up my table cloth, for the second time. Can you please get rid of it?"

The actual translation, as I wanted to appear literate enough to dine in such an elevated establishment, is: "Sir, if you take a look on my right, you will see a small creature climbing up the tablecloth. I tried to send it away to another table 5 minutes ago, but it apparently insists on returning here. It is obviously looking forward to sharing my rack of lamb with duchesse potatoes, and whereas I do congratulate it on its excellent choice, I'm not in the mood to share tonight. Can you convince him not to pursue this ill-conceived mission?"

The reason I didn't just say in French "can you please get rid of the cockroach" is because in polite conversation, French expressions are much more involved than English. Some of them are almost un-translatable, like the closing greeting in a letter where we say "Sincerely yours" the French way is: *Veuillez agréer Monsieur (or Madame) l'expression de mes sentiments les plus distingués*" ! Darn, I can't even translate this, it is of such hauteur! But basically it means, "Sincerely yours".

What followed was the most hysterical example of haute aristocratic chaos. The waiter straightened up as if he had been hit in the face and almost fell over backwards. The other horde of waiters hanging around in the center became alarmed at his sudden gesture which started a flurry of whispers among them, with discreet but alarming shots our way.

After a collective assessment of the situation, our waiter was designated as the front man to defuse the attack of the cockroach. He bent over to us and made some gestures indicating that the bug was being taken care of even though we couldn't see how since the bugger was still near my shoe. I think that they just tranquilized it to sit still until after dinner.

Needless to say, this all had to be done with acute aplomb so as not to disturb the rest of the diners. When it came time to get the check, they offered us a glass of champagne on the house. We thanked them for the generous gesture but declined, explaining that we were grateful that they didn't charge us extra for Monsieur Cafard. We paid the $475 bill and scurried away dans la nuit!

Back in New York, when we related this episode to Dennis, he broke out in a hysterical laughter, and wanted to call his former colleague in Paris and ask him about it but we dissuaded him. We felt is better to let sleeping roaches sleep. So much for Paris haute cuisine.

PINK RAT

After IBM, several of us former IBMers got together and formed a web development company called Pink Rat, LLC. The name came from our nicknames at IBM when many of the marketing people referred to us as the lab rats because we defined the architecture of the web marketing strategies which didn't always agree with the specific plans the marketing teams envisioned.

After all, certain things could be done, and certain other things could not be done. There were also legal issues. So in frustration they called us lab rats. But since we were 3 women at the beginning we accepted the slur by pointing out that while we might be lab rats, we were definitely Pink rats, as opposed to the Big Blue boys. It was all in good humor and everybody got along famously.

At Pink Rat we focused on small companies to give them an opportunity to enter this new big global market place. It wasn't always easy since these "companies", sometimes consisting of just 2 people, had no IT department and had as much knowledge of web architecture as the FGI ladies who thought the computer mouse was a sewing machine pedal.

But we managed to do it and over a period of 10 years, we developed dozens of websites, many in fashion, several in the entertainment field, various other companies in different industries, as well as several non-profit organizations and government projects. The Pink rats live on, though we're all turning kind of gray by now.

Letters

I DON'T QUITE KNOW HOW to explain this section other than to confess that sometimes when I felt that I needed to amuse myself, I would write letters to the editor of various publications, or companies with comments on their products. These were usually totally irrelevant but written in a serious tone regarding the most inconsequential issues, such as the number of cherries in a jar of jam.

I did sometimes get witty responses, like a shipment of preserved cherries. Well, some companies had a sense of humor.

The only serious exchange I did have at one time was with the New York Times because I am somewhat of a grammar nerd or grammarxist (is that a serious condition?) Anyway, my correspondence with the New York Times was of a more linguistic nature than just grammar. So here it is:

```
December 26, 1989


The Editor
The New York Times
229 West 43rd Street
New York, New York   10036

Dear Sir:

As Romania is in the process of turning a new leaf in its
identity, perhaps the New York Times will now reconsider the
spelling of this country's name.

Romania, derived from Roman, as in Roman Empire, has been
named thus by the Emperor Trajan during one of the numerous
invasions of this territory.  Previous to Roman occupation,
the area, despite loosely defined borders, was known as Dacia.

It is therefore perplexing to see the New York Times persist
with the RUMAN spelling, particularly when referring to proper
names such as the publication reported as **Rumania Literara**, in
your article "Bucharest Government Has Yet to Take Shape" of
December 25, 1989, page 14.

This is completely incorrect.  It is either **Literary Rumania**,
if one prefers an English translation (à la New York Times) or
**România Literară**, which is the correct Romanian spelling,
vowels, accents and all.

If the French newspaper La Libération, mentioned in the next
paragraph of this same article, merits its accent égu, surely
Romania deserves at least its historic and etymological O, if
not the accents.

Sincerely,


Renée Palmer
```

Figure 31 - Letter to the Editor, New York Times

And the response?

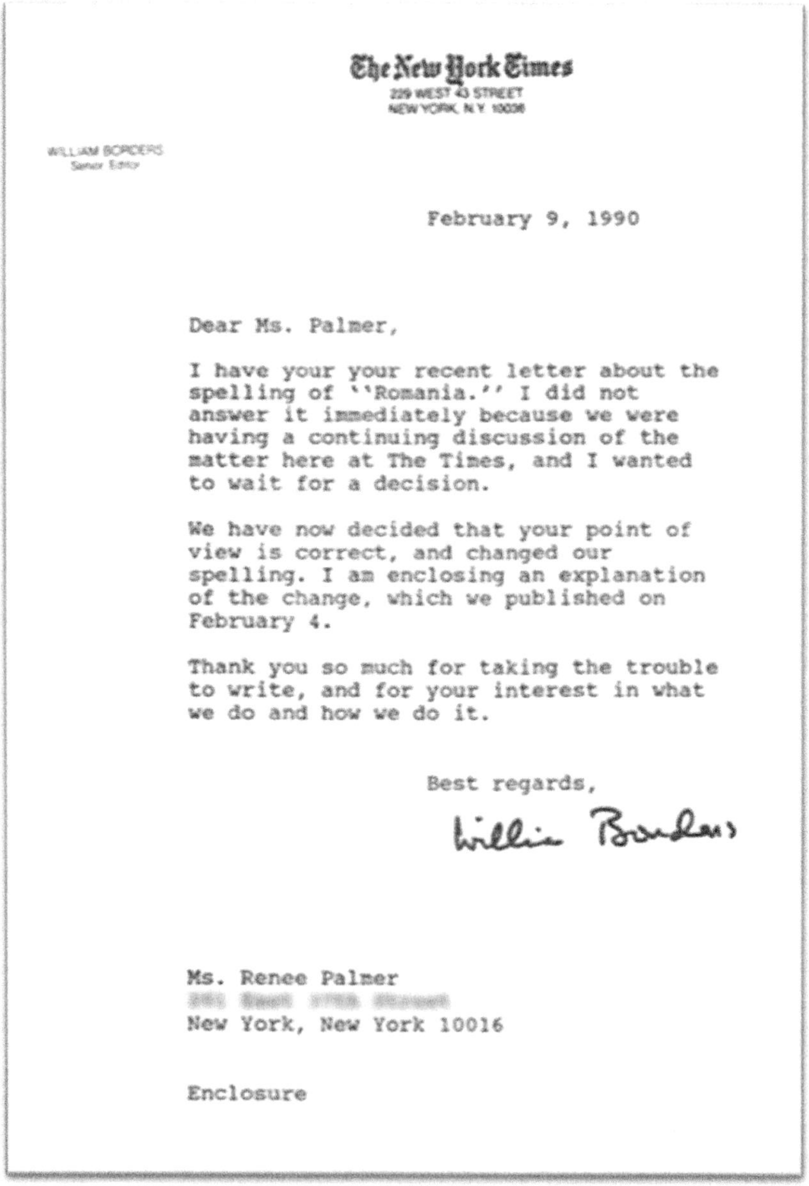

> **The New York Times**
> 229 WEST 43 STREET
> NEW YORK, N.Y. 10036
>
> WILLIAM BORDERS
> Senior Editor
>
> February 9, 1990
>
> Dear Ms. Palmer,
>
> I have your your recent letter about the spelling of ``Romania.'' I did not answer it immediately because we were having a continuing discussion of the matter here at The Times, and I wanted to wait for a decision.
>
> We have now decided that your point of view is correct, and changed our spelling. I am enclosing an explanation of the change, which we published on February 4.
>
> Thank you so much for taking the trouble to write, and for your interest in what we do and how we do it.
>
> Best regards,
>
> William Borders
>
> Ms. Renee Palmer
> New York, New York 10016
>
> Enclosure

Figure 32 – Response from the New York Times

Followed by this correction:

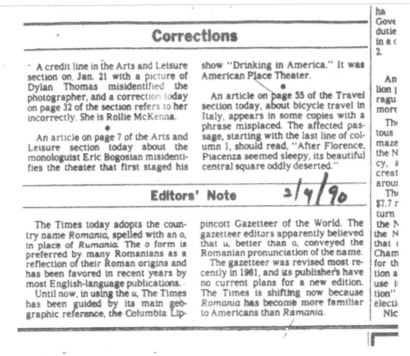

Figure 33 - New York Times correction

Score one for Romania!

Another letter to the New York Times had to do with my favorite columnist, Abe Rosenthal.

Sometime in 1994, I noticed that his column was not appearing on the editorial page so I called the newspaper to ask why the column was missing. I was told that he had a bad cold and was staying home for a few days.

Well, I decided that the best medicine for a cold is Romanian chicken soup so I wrote to him asking if he would like me to bring him some homemade chicken soup, and if yes, that I would be happy to drop it off at his apartment.

His answer was:

Figure 34 – Response from Abe Rosenthal, NY Times

And don't think he didn't enjoy it.

The New York Times
229 WEST 43 STREET
NEW YORK, N.Y. 10036

A. M. ROSENTHAL

December 13, 1994

Ms. Renee Palmer
201 East 37th Street
New York 10016

Dear Ms. Palmer,

    The soup was positively therapeutic -- as well as delicious. But most of all I'm grateful to you for your enormous kindness and thoughtfulness in thinking of me and delivering the soup right to my house! My wife and my sons join me in appreciation.

    I should be back at work writing very soon and your soup will be a reason for my speed.

Warmly,

Figure 35 – Response from Abe Rosenthal, NY Times

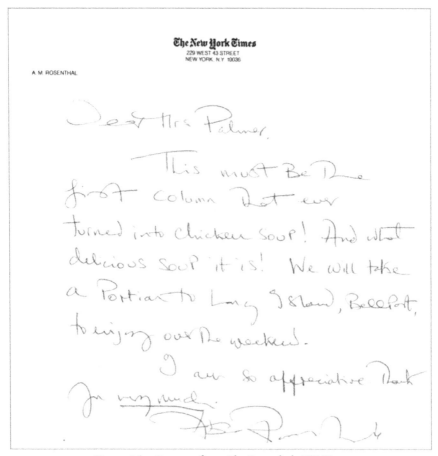

Figure 36 – Response from Abe Rosenthal, NY Times

I really miss Abe Rosenthal. And unfortunately, I never met him in person. It was one of those pen pal relationships.

Another New York Times columnist I always enjoyed back in the 1980s was Ron Alexander who had a column named *Metropolitan Diary* which published various submissions from readers, usually musings, poems, jokes - whatever.

So I submitted some thoughts about an issue that kept me perplexed which just goes to show how trivia can make you brain dead, or just hopelessly goofy.

Figure 37 – Letter to Metropolitan Diary

I never denied that my brain often took off to parts unknown. Or just locked down.

Personality traits

As I have been reflecting over many of the episodes described here, I came to realize that I have a bizarre personality trait which I must have inherited from my father. I can't seem to hold grudges against people who may have offended me or done something to harm me. My father was very much like this too – he never forgot good or bad things that happened, learned from them, and categorized people based on their actions. So even though he knew, for example, that some particular person was a treacherous evil person who may have hurt him, that never stopped him from being kind, polite, agreeable and even friendly with him. Of course he wouldn't trust him but despite any egregious act committed by such a person, he would never show his feelings. Therefore everybody adored my father – he never uttered a nasty or contentious comment to anybody, even to a sworn enemy. He considered holding grudges as a waste of time and an impediment to whatever his future plans were. So he never dwelled.

I'm very much like that, in fact, once somebody does something hurtful to me, they're out of my universe, but they never know it. In other words I tend to put people in a box so that I know their strengths and weaknesses and use them to my benefit. There's a term I think for this kind of attitude. I believe it's called Machiavellian.

I remember one time I had a crush on a guy when I was in college and after a few dates which I found very enjoyable, he declared that he didn't want to see me again. I don't remember what the reason was but I was upset. And the next week I had final exams so the timing was most inappropriate, for the spirit, at least. So what happened with my exams? I think it was the first semester where I got an A in every exam. He was so out of my universe, that nothing distracted me from preparing for the exams thus ending the year with nice bang. I did call him afterwards to tell him about my success thinking that it would make him mad. Instead, he wanted to celebrate by taking me to the theater so I got to see *Rosenkrantz and Guildenstern Are Dead* on his dime. Then I said good bye.

But back to more serious things - what was this other story about my father and the armoire?

Well, this was a bit more symbolic than literal, and frankly, the shock of my life!

Boy, was my father in an armoire!

It turns out, that my father had a double life that we did not find out about until 2013, some 65 years after it happened. This revelation was entirely due to gossip, possibly the most effective revelation of all secrets.

It happened about a month after I came back from a trip to Romania in May 2013 when I went to visit my home town with my cousin Neomy (Zisi). She hadn't been there in 50 years, and I hadn't been there since my last trip from France, in 1972. We used to live across the street from each other in Borşa and Neomy kept in contact with a family friend, Sava, who was going to be our guide in trying to locate our old friends.

So in 2013 with Neomy, other than revisiting this place which was no longer a one street village with little houses, never bigger than 1 or 2 stories, we started looking up some of our childhood friends. Borşa was now a real city with apartment buildings, supermarkets, stores and other businesses that did not exist 50 years ago. It didn't look anything like the village I remembered.

But the most enjoyable aspect of this trip was of course discovering some old friends whom we hadn't seen in over 50 years. One such friend was my former next door neighbor Emilia, the one with whose pigs I used to sleep. It was just wonderful to see her, her brother and all the other long lost friends. I also saw my friend Stela in whose house I fainted because I thought ghosts from the cemetery were knocking on the window. It was a trip full of laughs in recalling our old adventures.

A few weeks after I got back to New York, I got a Skype call from my cousin Neomy from Israel who told me that she got a call from her friend Sava in Borşa who told her that my friend Emilia discovered an incredible secret about my family and she was afraid to contact me directly, so she went around to Sava, who then called my cousin who then called me and who was now hesitating telling me what this was about because I was going through a bit of a rough time with various crises here in New York.

As I was relating some of these crappy events to my cousin, she said that maybe this was not a good time to tell me some "interesting" news. Of course, the minute somebody says something like that, your ears perk up like a cat's and basically you start foaming at the mouth with curiosity. At least that was my reaction.

I mean, who doesn't like gossip? So what was the "interesting" news? Apparently after we left Borşa, my former neighbor Emilia called a friend of hers, who had moved to Germany several years ago. I knew this friend, Viorica, because we all used to play together when we were kids.

Among other things, Emilia said to her, "Guess who was here in Borşa last month?" To which Viorica answered, of course, "Who?" Emilia said, "Renee Schneider, remember her?" Silence at the other end. So Emilia asked, "Hello, are you there?" Answer: "Yes, I'm sitting down, catching my breath".

And then it came out. Viorica was speechless and confessed that she had been carrying a secret since her mother revealed it to her on her deathbed, 10 years earlier. She never told anyone about it, mainly because she didn't even know if I was alive and if so, where I lived, or any other information since, as I said, I never kept in touch with any of my old friends after I left in 1962.

So what did her mother confess on her death bed? That I was her half-sister!!!

Imagine the shock. Her mother had never married so Viorica never knew who her father was. Also, the life we led in Romania at that time was always full of secrets. And it wasn't just Jews, it was basically a society full of secrets, especially where it concerned children. Nothing like today when things are explained to children that they probably shouldn't even know about until they're grown up. But that's what it was like at that time plus this was definitely a scandal of some magnitude.

Apparently my father had an affair with her mother when I was 1 year old and nobody knew about it. Her mother was living with us as a housekeeper but mostly as a baby sitter because my mother was not very capable of taking care of me as a baby. I was a difficult and dangerous birth and my mother simply couldn't cope. But my mother must have suspected something because she fired her and Viorica was born a year later but nobody knew anything about her father.

Figure 39 - Viorica, Emilia, Zoia, Renee and Gheza, Emilia's brother, circa 1954

So after 55 years she found out that her childhood friend Renee was her half-sister and I found out 10 years later that one of my childhood friends is my half-sister.

I thought she was just another kid in the neighborhood and she was always at my cousin Zoia's house, the one who shared the house with us. In fact, here we are around 1954. !

How much crazier can life get?

It was the most unbelievable news. I couldn't sleep for several days. I told Shari who was also gap mouthed and we just couldn't figure out how such a secret could be kept right under our noses, for so many years.

I met my half-sister Viorica first on Skype together with her husband and her 2 lovely daughters. It is very hard to explain the feeling. We talked and talked and talked and I found out a lot of details about our life at the time that I didn't know about.

Apparently, my father's family took care of both her and her mother so they didn't suffer from any deprivations, especially since her mother never married and there were no jobs available.

I also found out that before we left Romania in 1962, my father went to Borșa to their house and met with her mother in front of the house, though he never went in. He apparently gave her money because Viorica told me that all of a sudden they bought a cow, and wood and other necessities and her mother got a job at the office of my father's friend. But her mother never told her who the man was that came to their house.

And here we are, in Munich, the 3 sisters in May 2015.

Figure 40 - The 3 sisters: Shari, Viorica, Renee, May 2015

How's that for a shocker?

Perhaps this is what I was waiting for to finish what I started in 1997. I went full circle. If I hadn't gone back to my hometown, after some 40+ years, I would have never found out about this new family member.

Life is full of surprises, isn't it?

Takeaway

WHAT WAS THE PURPOSE OF all this ink?

Aside from chronicling historical events which I think every culture needs to document for future generations, it is important to learn from the past even if society and culture change and perhaps precisely because society changes.

In my case it was strictly a case of adapting to changes that were all unsettling upheavals, but I was always about being open to new experiences. The fact that I never had any ambitions in life about anything, whether career or family or any other aspect of living in a modern society probably prevented me from accomplishing more on any particular level.

Since I had no special drive or talent, I always admired people who did have visible talents or interests and pursued them. I had none. In fact, to be very honest, I never actually understood why anyone had to "work". Ok, I figured out that, unless you live in a hut in the wilderness, you need money to pay the rent and buy food so the money has to come from somewhere but I really found work to be simply a means to an end. To what end? After disposing of typical financial obligations, the main goal was finding ways to amuse myself, because if I had to describe myself in one word, I would say "goofy".

It is therefore important to know who you are and why you are the way you are, to accept it and to be aware of your strength, your limitations and your influence and the effect of your behavior and personality on the people that surround you. My interest in amusing myself definitely comes from my father. He was always amused – he amused himself and us. No matter how dark things were, he always had something silly or funny to say that lifted the darkness and raised hope.

One other thing I inherited from my father was an impatience with details and disregard for minutiae, or as my father used say – "peste meinses", which is something like "useless trivia". Such as wasting time to buy a wedding dress – just get married and get on with it. This is what he actually said to me. I guess that's how I ended mistaking a prom dress for a wedding gown.

So what do I think about my father's scandalous transgression 65 years ago? After the shock, I just smiled like a Cheshire cat! I wish he were still around to tell him what I found out. I cannot imagine what his response would have been. I hope he wouldn't have discounted it as just some more trivia. Unfortunately, I'll never know.

What did I inherit from my mother besides her face?

Figure 41 - Who's who at age 14?

The tendency to panic when something is not quite as I imagine it should be. Like the time she took me to the doctor when I was baby because … I didn't cry. Babies cry so if I didn't cry, it meant there was something wrong with me. The doctor reassured her that there was nothing wrong, I was just a happy baby. Duh! But then she may have had a not unreasonable concern since I was a breach baby who had to be smacked severely before I uttered a cry at birth.

On the other hand, I had no such reason for concern when I took my cat to the vet because he didn't meow. The vet asked me if he ever meowed and I said no. So he told me to go home, lock the cat in a closet for an hour. I did. He meowed after about 15 minutes.

Therefore, my strong belief in nature and nurture cannot be shaken because it is a scientific fact.

We are the product of our upbringing and of the society in which we were brought up. Although I was brought up in a loving family, the fact that my parents could not protect me from various abuses typical of totalitarian regimes, I learned that I could never count on anybody but myself for survival. Nothing really wrong with that - makes you strong and creative in defining your own survival tactics. In my case, a sense of humor (to feed my need for self-amusement) always worked to my advantage. Life is to be enjoyed; I think my motto has always been, "Lighten up".

But a life of secrets is just not fair to children. My family's secrets deprived me of knowing about my half-sister. And if it wasn't for her mother's deathbed confessions, we would have never known about each other. How fair is that?

I always liked surprises, no matter how silly they were, even when based on mistakes. I mean what's the big deal about dragging a heavy suitcase of books through a snow storm in the Carpathian mountains and finding out that the suitcase actually contained a pig?

Cluj-Napoca, 2013

*** The End ***

Acknowledgements

There are several people I need to thank for their help in reminding me of various details, dates, suggestions, edits and other helpful hints.

I first want to thank Tinuţa Grec from the Biblioteca Orășeneasca Borșa (Borșa City Library) who detailed our family's life in the fabulous history book about Borșa -***RĂDĂCINI*** – *O Istorie a Borșei în Imagini, 1914-2014 Volumul II*

I want to thank Bess Heitner, the talented jewelry designer who was an editor in a previous life and who pointed out some gaps in some of the narratives; Loredana Giacca, a former Hermès colleague who knows more about the Hermès family than any current or past employee and clarified some details I had forgotten about; Miles Cahn, former owner of Coach Leatherware who also clarified some details I no longer remembered; Patricia Maffei from the Fashion Group International who helped me research fashion information in FGI's archives.

I want to thank my cousin Neomy Fruchter who, while traveling with me through the beautiful countryside on our Romanian adventures in 2013 and 2014, gave me new information about her father, my father's twin brother; during these two trips we untangled a lot of mysteries.

I want to thank the remaining members of my mother's family who gave me invaluable information about their experiences before and during the Holocaust: my uncle Eugene Davis, who in his mid-90s is still sharp as a tack and who gave me amazing details about his and his brother's journeys during the Holocaust.

With much regret, I want to thank posthumously my aunt Joan Ferencz, who weeks before her sudden passing, also gave me remarkable details about some of her and her sisters' experiences in the camps.

I must also thank the USC Shoah Foundation, *The Institute for Visual History and Education,* for giving me permission to post the short clip of my mother's interview. For people who want to hear some of these stories from survivors, there is no better forum for viewing some of these testimonies. https://sfi.usc.edu/vha/about

Last but not least, I want to thank my husband, Shelly for putting up with having to read the endless revisions and restraining himself from correcting every instance of what he calls my "franglais" syntax. He's a lawyer and I think a reincarnation of Edwin Newman because he's mercilessly fierce about proper English which is not my strength considering that I have to speak 3 different languages daily with my friends and relatives in different countries.

References

- List of women prisoners Oct 1944 in Auschwitz: http://palmerny.com/cs/AUSCHWITZ.pdf
- Our photos at the Holocaust Museum: https://www.youtube.com/watch?v=awF09iGP6Jo
- Excerpt from the Shoah Foundation interview of my mother, Caroline Schneider: https://youtu.be/nO9mc-d2Udo

Made in the USA
Columbia, SC
27 November 2018